To

Randy's
#Noah
Margaret

Barbara Bush

OH MY DOG!

Personal Stories of How Dogs Enrich Our Lives

by

Barbara Berlier

Tail-Wag Publishing © 2019

**TAIL WAG
PUBLISHING**
Arizona, USA

ISBN-13: 9781071100189
ISBN-10: 1071100189

For more information about permission to reproduce selections from
this book, please contact the author at:

2418 Topanga Dr
Bullhead City, AZ 86442

FIRST EDITION
TAIL WAG PUBLISHING™

Cover design by Rocky Berlier

Book design and layout by Rocky Berlier
www.concierge-publishing.com

Manufactured in the United States of America

Dedications

I dedicate this book to my sister, Ann, who has selflessly devoted her life to the welfare of animal rescue and continues to be the voice of those who have no voice. Thank you for inviting me on this amazing journey.

To *mon petit frere* (my little brother) Rocky, without whom this book would never had been possible. Thank you.

To the love of my life, my husband, Paul for always encouraging me to be the best version of myself.

To my sweet Lady Sarah, for being the inspiration behind every story written here.

Contributors

Ann Herrington – Prior owner/publisher of Prescott Dog magazine and current Owner/Publisher of Tucson Dog magazine: *"A Tribute to Bernie, The Prescott Dog, a Shelter Dog Story"*

Dane Hays – A highly decorated retired military man and hero: *"Nowzad: Dogs of Afghanistan"*, *"War Dogs: The Forgotten Soldiers"*

George Hammond – *"The Tired Stranger"*

Baron Von Threetoes Jackson – *"A Letter from a sled dog in Alaska, the happiest dog in the world"*

Connie Newman – *"Queen Geena"*

Acknowledgments

A special 'thank you' to all of the following people for opening their homes and their hearts to share their amazing and heartfelt stories with me:

Sandra Anglin • Virginia Cameron • Thea Dorman • Maryse Dunn • Barbara Evans • Mary Goulette • Jack and Carol Hakim • Sally Harris • Dane Hays • Marlys Hastings • Kent and Sharon Jewell • Jim and Sandy King • Julia Klausner • Jean Krietemeyer • Lenny Lu Lambert • Lucky and Donna Lovitt • Herb and Mary Macy • Jack Mantie • Tom and Lorean Michaels • Don and Pat McNiven • Bob and Judy Newman • Dave and Marie Newman • Robert and Barbara Olson • Peggy Pate • Ray and Pat Patterson • Shell Pelismo • Gene and Jane Richardson • Hilde Riedel • Phillip Welicky • and...

ADDITIONALLY:

- ❖ 'Pepper' at Margaret T. Morris Center, Prescott, Arizona,
- ❖ Bring your Dog to Work Day (celebrating 20 years on July 20, 2019
- ❖ Prescott Valley Samaritan Center
- ❖ Adult Center of Prescott Community
- ❖ Think4inc

Contents

✒

The Tired Stranger

by George Hammond

An older, tired looking dog wandered into my yard one day. I could tell from his collar and well-fed belly that he had a home, and was well cared for. He calmly came over to me, I gave him a few pats on his head, he then followed me into my house, slowly walked down the hall, curled up in the corner and fell asleep. An hour later, he went to the door and I let him out. The next day he was back, greeted me in my yard, walked inside, resumed his spot in the hall, and again slept for about an hour. This continued off and on for several weeks. Curious, I pinned a note to his collar, *"I would like to find out who the owner is of this wonderful sweet dog, and ask if you are aware that almost every afternoon your dog comes to my house for a nap?"*

The next day he arrived for his nap, with a different note pinned on his collar, *"He lives in a home with six children, two under the age of three, and he's trying to catch up on his sleep. Can I come with him tomorrow?"*

"Dogs are always good and full of selfless love.
They are undiluted vessels of joy who never, ever,
deserve anything bad that happens to them."
~ Steven Rowley

A Tribute to 'Bernie,'
From THE PRESCOTT DOG:
A Shelter Dog Story

by Ann Herrington

Our kinship and reverence for animals is as old as human history; we have bonded with them for thousands of years. They give us unconditional love, loyalty and devotion, even risking their lives to save ours. Our shared understanding has grown over the years so that animals have become part of our families. We have grown in our ability to respect and protect them, which is the least they deserve after all that they give us.

In early December 2015, during a routine visit to the vet, they found an anal sac carcinoma growing inside *"Bernie."* My wonderful veterinarian, Dr. Batt, looked at me with pain in her eyes as she told me his diagnosis. I felt like I was in the Twilight Zone, hearing the words from an alternate universe. Out of nowhere, and without any warning signs, my sweet boy had cancer; the most aggressive type too.

I spent all of December working with Dr. Batt, as well as with my loving holistic veterinarian, Dr. Delia MacDonald. I also took him to an oncologist in Scottsdale, to no avail.

Bernie passed away the day after Christmas. His life was cut short at 8 years. I was devastated; I still am. However, I'm now focusing on all we did together, all the memories we shared, and all our success with helping shelter animals. Bernie was a shelter dog who was always by my side. This is our story.

Bernie was *one in a million* and my love for him, as well as his for me, was boundless. Our connection was very deep, like nothing I have ever experienced. I have loved other dogs but never like him; he got me! We could talk to each other without saying a word. We read each other's thoughts. He understood almost everything I said and listened intently as I spoke to him. He was the sweetest soul I have ever known, and became my heart, the mascot and the soul of my magazine, The Prescott Dog.

Anatole France said, *"Until one has loved an animal, a part of one's soul remains unawakened."* Bernie awakened my soul and taught me patience, joy, and most importantly, how to live *in* and *for* the moment.

He was the founding dog and canine writer for The Prescott Dog. Like his feature column, *"Bernie Barks,"* he always wanted to help people and other animals. We were on a mission together, to tell everyone about how wonderful shelter dogs are and how much joy they must bring to their families.

When I look into the eyes of a shelter or rescue dog, I see my sweet boy and remember the blessed day he came to live with me. And like many shelter dogs, Bernie had gone through several homes before coming to me. Did you know that the average dog has 3 homes in his/her life? Such was the case with Bernie.

Bernie was brought to Prescott Animal Control (PAC) before the Yavapai Humane Society took over. Things were bleaker for animals in those days. Luckily for Bernie, United Animal Friends went to the shelter and brought dogs out to *"adopt-a-thons"* at different pet-related stores. Bernie was taken to Pet Headquarters in Prescott Valley and shown for adoption.

My friend Pete was driving by Pet Headquarters and saw some dogs for adoption out front. He was not looking for another dog that day; he and his wife Lorri already had Sophie, a cute, sweet French bulldog. But when Pete saw Bernie, he knew he was special. He went home to tell Lorri and she fell in love too.

Bernie was about 6 months old and it appeared that he had *kennel cough, which is* an illness that affects the respiratory-tract of dogs. It is very contagious and is commonly found in dogs that are frequently around other dogs at places like boarding facilities and doggy daycare. If he was brought back to the shelter, he would have most likely been euthanized to prevent the spread of the disease through the shelter, which would put every animal at risk.

My friends really loved and cared for Bernie, with Pete spending hours playing ball with him, and Lorri taking him on walks every day. Their French bulldog, Sophie, also loved Bernie as she played with him every day, even though he was so much bigger than her. He was so gentle with her and would let her do anything she wanted to him. He had the best disposition like that.

In April of 2008, I lost my first shelter dog, "Harley," a Dalmatian. He had introduced me to animal shelters and the plight of these poor animals in 1997 when I went to adopt a friend for my other Dalmatian, "Haley." Sadly, Haley had passed away before I moved to Prescott, but Harley was with me until he was 12 years old. He had many health problems, and it was painful to let him go.

When my friends had taken in Bernie, he was about 18 months old. When they heard of my loss of Harley, and the struggle I was having with it, Lorri called me to see if I might want a visit from Bernie, who she said was so sweet and would make me feel better. I was hesitant but agreed saying, *"Well, ok, but I'm not keeping him"* and the next day, Bernie came over with his food and all his toys. Suffice to say, he never left and that began our incredible life together.

When I got Bernie, everything changed. I felt happy again and because of him, I launched **The Prescott Dog** in 2008. During that time, I took a job in hospice where the owners were big animal lovers and allowed us to bring our dogs to work.

Bernie went to work with me every day and became the office mascot, walking around visiting all the employees, and sometimes enticing them into a game of ball. The General Manager taught him to place the ball up on her desk, so she could throw it to him. He never forgot that, and I think some of the other employees wished she hadn't taught him that! He was a great mood elevator to a lot of people, especially me, and having him with me every day was a dream come true.

One day, I took Bernie with me to the inpatient unit where a lady, who was visiting with her mom—a patient—asked if Bernie could come in and visit with them. He walked right in the room, and that was the beginning of Bernie visiting patients and their families on a regular basis.

Bernie loved everyone and was always very attentive to people's emotions. Like he did for me, Bernie made other people *"feel better."* So much so, that he eventually became a registered therapy dog. He always knew who needed him, and I witnessed him sitting with people many times, quietly loving and comforting them. The nurses even began requesting that Bernie be brought over to spend time with certain patients.

It really was the most amazing thing I have ever seen and so fulfilling. If we humans could only communicate like dogs do! They know the right things to do without being able to say a word.

Bernie and I also attended the Bradshaw Mountain Special Olympics and brought many of our therapy dog friends there to meet and greet the Olympians in the Pavilion and keep them company while they waited for their turn to compete. We marched in the parade with them in the opening ceremonies, and it was an exhilarating day for everyone! What a gift these special animals are and how lucky we are to have them.

We had so many adventures together. I took him to the beach for the first time in 2012. I needed a break, so I rented a little apartment just blocks from the Pacific Dog Beach in San Diego, California. Bernie was a natural and loved every moment of it. He ran in the water, romping with other dogs and playing for hours. I could barely drag him away, he loved it so much. He wrote about his *"summer vacation"* in his feature column *"Bernie Barks"*, with lots of great pictures. I will never forget that trip!

Another beach trip included Bernie's BFF, Savannah, my daughter's black Lab. At Rocky Point Mexico, they romped on the beach for days. Obviously, Bernie was a beach bum!

Bernie was a Frisbee freak too! He knew how to play ball but one day, my friend Jill and I decided to try him with a Frisbee. Two throws and he figured it out and he never stopped. He wanted to play every day, all day. People used to laugh at his laser beam focus on that Frisbee as he never took his eyes off it as you were getting ready to throw it, and rarely ever missed catching it! He was a great athlete. We took agility classes and he did well with that too.

People sometimes feel guilty about having to euthanize their beloved pet. *"Did I do the right thing? Maybe I should have waited."* What I realized is that whatever we do, our pet understands that we love them, and are making the very best decision for them that we can out of that love. They understand, especially when it comes to pain and lack of a quality of life.

Bernie was full of life and that awful disease took it from him. Saying goodbye was the worst thing I ever had to do. We have the right to grieve their loss in whatever way we want and for however long it takes. Although that is heartbreaking, we need to remember to celebrate their lives and all that they have taught us. I truly believe they are our spiritual teachers. They love us unconditionally, validate us and enrich our lives in so many ways.

I think shelter dogs know that we saved them and, like the car magnet I have seen that says, *"Who saved who?"*, they often are the ones that really (ultimately) save us from a lonely life, a life without unconditional love, a life without joy or fun. They teach us to be present in the moment, the way they live.

I try never to say *"never"* but I don't know that I will ever have a dog again, especially one like Bernie. He was so smart, so loving, so much fun, and he seemed to always be smiling, and so was I when I was with him. He motivated me and made me want to be a better human being because I wanted to be as good as he was.

When I think of him today, I think of the story from my favorite book, **The Art of Racing in the Rain by Garth Stein**. The book is told from the perspective of *"Enzo,"* the dog, who tells us, *"In Mongolia, when a dog dies, he is buried high in the hills so people cannot walk on his grave. The dog's master whispers into the dog's ear his wish that the dog will return as a man in his next life."*

Not all dogs return as men they say, only those who are ready. Enzo says, *"I am ready."* He knows he is different from other dogs, a philosopher with a nearly human soul. That was my Bernie, he seemed almost human to me, and he understood pretty much everything I said. He was incredible.

Although Bernie is gone, I will never forget him and all he taught me. I know he is still around and visits me often in my dreams. My goal is to continue the mission that he and Harley taught me about shelter dogs, cats, and equines; to continue spreading that word as far as I can and as long as I am breathing.

These animals end up in shelters through no fault of their own. I would like to ask for your help in continuing this mission with me by supporting rescue and shelter organizations, and to spread the word about how important it is to spay & neuter, as well as to adopt from a shelter or rescue group. Whether is it is through financial support or volunteering, you can make a difference…we did.

So, hug your fur babies tonight just a little tighter, and tell them how much you love them, as you just never know what fate has in store for you tomorrow.

I love you and miss you more than I can say my beloved boy, but I know I will see you again when it is my time. You were pure love and it was my greatest joy that you let me share your life!

When Bernie was at the end, we traveled to Las Vegas to spend Christmas with all our family not realizing that he would not make it back with me. We were very fortunate to find Dr. Toby Goldman from LAP OF LOVE VETERINARY HOSPICE. He was so loving, patient, kind and provided the most peaceful passing for Bernie, surrounded by our family at my daughter's home there. Dr. Toby gave me a beautiful book with so many loving ideas to celebrate Bernie's life and some wonderful poems. Thank you to, LAP OF LOVE, for giving me permission to share one of them with you. It has given me great comfort.

My Dear Family,

Today, I am as I was meant to be: young, energetic, full of life and able to explore everything around me. My legs work perfectly, there is no more pain and I can run, jump and play with all my friends. Most of all, there is no regret, no aging and no confusion.

I ask that you not grieve for the loss of what we shared but rejoice in the fact that we lived and loved each other with unconditional adoration. One touch or kiss from you, one pat on the head, one favorite read, was all that was needed for a lifetime of unwavering commitment from me to love you and cherish you until my time had come. I am grateful and thankful that our lives merged and we were able to share such special moments together.

I will await your arrival as we are always meant to be together. Please do not hold on to the love that you shared with me but share it with another so that I may live on forever in your heart. Remember, to have loved and lost is better than to have never loved at all.

With Unconditional Love,

~Your Angel

Where Sarah Used to Live

*"Did you ever notice when you blow in a dog's face
he gets mad at you? But when you take him in a car
he sticks his head out the window."* ~ Steve Bluestone

Sarah was a Christmas present from my husband Paul in 1986, the year we got married. She was a Cocker Spaniel, with a silky red coat, long droopy ears, that she often stepped on, sad brown eyes and a white marking from the top of her head to the tip of her nose. She was perfect! I laugh now remembering how Paul explained to me what the rules were. *"Dogs don't belong on the bed,"* he said, *"we have to train her properly."* So, we put up a gate to the master bathroom and put plenty of paper on the floor; we were going to show her who was in charge. Within one week she had trained us. She was not only *on* the bed, she was *under* the covers. And so, life with Lady Sarah had begun.

Let me say right here that I always called her either Lady or Sarah, unless she was in trouble, and then I called her by her full name, Lady Sarah. What is amazing is that she knew the difference. She loved going for walks to the park, and she loved being around the grandkids; and they loved her too. She particularly liked being around the kids when cookies were handed out. She would bark at company when they came in and wouldn't stop until they acknowledged her. She was very social. The night of January 16, 1994 was a particularly hot night, even for California. In the weeks that had proceeded this night, Sarah had begun digging in the house. We would come home from work to find pillows from the couch and bed all over the floor. I thought it a bit strange, but I just figured she had acquired a new bad habit.

I had a terrible time getting to sleep that night, besides being hot; Sarah decided she wanted to sleep on my pillow, right next to my head. I tried to push her away, but to no avail. Finally, I drifted off to sleep. Then at 4:37AM, on the morning of January 17, 1994, the world started to shake, and it seemed like it would never stop. The Northridge Earthquake was reported as a 6.7 magnitude, and we felt every bone-rattling shake of it.

My husband told me later that Sarah was licking my face profusely while I was screaming, and she never left my side. When the shaking finally stopped, we had lost almost everything we owned, but we were just grateful that we all got out with our lives.

Later, when we were somewhat over the shock of what happened, we remembered about Sarah and her digging. My family and I are convinced that Sarah *knew* the quake was coming. As a confirmation of this, with no more earthquakes in the ensuing months, her digging stopped!

With our apartment destroyed, we searched for, and finally found, a new home that we fell in love with. It was on a huge lot with a swimming pool and several fruit trees; we moved in April of 1994. Sarah loved the new home too.

One of the first things I had to do was to show her where the steps were in the pool, just in case she would decide to take a midnight swim or accidentally fall in. And it's a good thing we did!

One winter night, about 2 AM, my husband and I both were bolted out of bed by the shock of a cold wet mattress. There, under the covers, was a sopping wet Sarah. We surmised that she must have fallen in the pool. Sarah looked at us as if to say, *"why are you guys looking at me like that?"* She provided us with many great memories.

Around the middle of October of 1999, Sarah got very sick. Our veterinarian, Doctor Gilmore, gave us some medication and special food for her; he told us that she had an enlarged liver. At first the medication and food seemed to make a difference. Sarah seemed to be getting better; even playing in the yard with the squirrels again. However, she could no longer jump up on the bed to be with us. So, I laid a pillow on the floor for her to sleep on, next to my side of the bed. She found her comfort there, and I would hang my hand over the side, so she could feel me there.

One morning I got up for work, went to get my cup of tea, and realized that Sarah was not behind me. This was unusual because she always got up and walked to the kitchen with me in the morning. However, this time, she lay there on the pillow, still sleeping. I put her daily dog treat on her pillow, hoping that when I got home that night, she would be awake and happy to see me as always.

That evening I went straight home after work. I opened the door and immediately knew something was very wrong. For the last 13 years, Sarah had met me at the door whenever I came home. I ran to my room and saw her, still on the pillow where I had left her.

As she lay there, I felt a knot in the pit in my stomach. With Sarah's age and health, I just knew that I was facing some difficult decisions. The thought of her suffering panicked me. I picked her up in her blanket, looked at my husband, and without either of us speaking a word, we jumped in the car and drove to our veterinarian's office.

When we got there Sarah was very quiet, she licked my hand, almost as if to say, *"it's okay, you can let me go."* My husband and I comforted her; staying with her as she peacefully slipped away.

I hugged Lady Sarah with tears flowing from my eyes, then leaning over, I whispered to her, *"I will see you again at the Rainbow Bridge."*

Coming home from work after Sarah was gone was the hardest part of any day for me. Her absence only emphasized how empty our house was now. It was so sad that she would no longer be there to greet me in our daily routine together. It's amazing how much a part of our lives she had become. She was family and losing her was like losing a family member.

One night, I was alone in the living room watching TV and I heard a noise in the kitchen; it sounded like Sarah's dog tags hitting her metal dish. And for just that moment, I forgot she was gone.

I still miss her companionship, her acceptance, and the unconditional love that only a sweet pet like her can provide. In the time we had together, she made me want to be a better human, and to do extraordinary things for animals. So, for now, I walk a little slower from the car to the house, and there's a hole in my heart where Sarah used to live.

"I have sometimes thought of the final cause of dogs having such short lives And I am quite satisfied it is in compassion to humans; For if we suffer so much in losing a dog after ten or twelve years, what would it be if they were to double that time." ~ Sir Walter Scott

A Courageous Man
and Two Exceptional Dogs

"A dog has no use for fancy cars, or big homes, or designer clothes. Status symbols mean nothing to him. A waterlogged stick will do just fine. A dog judges others not by their color or creed or class, but by who they are inside. A dog doesn't care if you are rich or poor, educated or illiterate, clever or dull. Give him your heart and he will give you his. It was quite simple really, and yet we humans, so much wiser and more sophisticated, have always had trouble figuring out what really counts and what does not."
~ 'Marley and Me' by John Grogan.

Dane Hays moved to Prescott Valley in February 2009, he lives at GRAYSON HOUSE, an assisted care facility, with his companion *"Pooh,"* a beautiful Border Collie/ Australian Shepherd mix. As we talked about his extraordinary journey here, I was taken aback by his gentle demeanor. He was soft-spoken and yet very open about his life. Dane served his country for 20 years in the Army holding several positions including Special Ops and Special Ops Recruiter. In 1991 he retired due to injuries he suffered in the line of duty.

One day, when leaving the recruiting office, he became a victim of a vicious attack; so severely beaten that the attackers left him for dead. The EMT's and Doctors called his time of death twice. Dane told me with a modest chuckle, *"I guess I survived because I was too stubborn to die."* While he certainly survived the attack, his prognosis was not very good. The attackers had severely damaged his body and, to a large degree, his spirit.

He spent his long recovery at Fort Hood, Texas. Speaking of his time there he said, *"One of the (many) therapists I had at Fort Hood told me that if I didn't challenge myself, I would never get better."* Any other man might have given in to this badly injured body and shaken soul, but this man was extraordinary. Heeding the warning of his therapist, he started pushing himself in numerous ways to challenge both his body and spirit. He decided to volunteer at a homeless shelter and spent three years at it in Phoenix.

In 1993, Dane attended a conference in Washington DC where he represented a Health Care Company from Phoenix, then as a Health Care Advocate working with the Clintons for four years. Dane said he has very fond memories of his time there.

Dane bought a motor home in 1997 where he began an eight-year adventure of touring the country. I asked him what place stood out in his mind and he said, "there were so many beautiful places, but Alaska is just incredible; so much so that I would love to go there again.

After a year of traveling alone, he decided he needed a travel companion. So, he went to the Yavapai Humane Society and there he found *"Buzz"*, a three-month-old Border Collie/ Shepherd mix, who turned out to be an enthusiastic traveler.

Speaking with an air of pride, he said, *"Buzz was of exceptional intelligence. He was trained as a service dog and he learned very quickly, and was eager to please. Buzz instinctively knew when I was having a medical problem. He was always happy, and was a truly special companion to me."*

Unfortunately, in 2005 his travels were cut short as Dane suffered two heart attacks and the doctors told him they found that he had a 70% blockage in his heart. And, of course, the injuries that he had sustained from the attack also contributed to his failing health. Buzz was always by his side, offering comfort and love. *"In November of 2008 Buzz became very ill."* Dane said sorrowfully. *"He was found to have a faulty heart valve; his health began to quickly deteriorate. For all that he had done for me, now I had to make the most difficult decision a human must make for their dear companion. On December 2008 I held Buzz for one last time while he peacefully slipped away."* He added, *"After Buzz passed away, I had a hard time sleeping as he had always been there by my side; my constant companion."*

Missing Buzz and the companionship he brought, Dane call the Yavapai Humane Society again. *"Dawn Gonzales told me she would keep an eye out for that special dog that would fit my life."* He said. *"Then One day I got a call from Dawn and she said there was a dog that was just dropped off that I might be interested in. Dawn also said not to be put off by her appearance as she had been terribly neglected. It was a miracle she had survived being tied up and left outside for two years. Her toenails were so long that they had curled up under her paws. She was so sweet and starved for attention. I told Dawn to bring her over for me to meet."*

"When I saw her, she looked like a big ball of dust with two beady little eyes and I immediately fell in love with her. "Pooh", as I named her, is a Border Collie/Australian Shepherd mix and it was uncanny how much she looked like Buzz." As a grin came over his face he said, *"She is a natural clown and loves people, considering all she had gone through, it was a miracle that she would be so trusting. When I go to the dinner hall, I park my wheelchair outside the door and leave Pooh there. She has become the professional greeter. Most everyone smiles and says "hello," then pats her on the head, and, of course, she just eats that up. Even those that have become withdrawn will smile and give her a pat."*

It sounds like Pooh has become an ambassador of Good Will at Grayson House. It seems only right that these two, who have been through so much, would find and comfort each other. Dane is so appreciative that Grayson House is an animal friendly facility. It really is therapeutic for so many of the elderly who look forward to their daily visit with Pooh.

When asking Dane about his life today, he told me, *"At least twice a month Pooh and I go boating at Lake Powell. She is not afraid of anything; she loves taking the boat out and absolutely loves the water. In fact, it's hard keeping her in the boat. I take Pooh for a 3-mile walk once a week; this helps to build up her leg muscles. I am also trying to teach her some games; no one had ever played with her, so she doesn't yet understand how to play, but we're getting there."*

I would like to thank Dane Hays for being so forth coming about his life and his service to this country; also, to Grayson House for all that they do for their seniors. For Dane and Pooh, we hope you both will enjoy many more adventures.

UPDATE: A LETTER FROM DANE

Barbara,

So much has changed and improved in my life and I wanted to let you know. In September 2009 my physical strength increased, and I was finally able to function without the power chair, just using a cane. We (Pooh and I) left Grayson and moved to Cordes Lakes. I progressed so well that, in just a few months, I was able to get around without the cane. We were able to go back to Grayson to visit a few times, but sadly most of the people we knew there had passed away.

We have a new home with lots of room which challenges me physically, yet the endeavor has helped heal my body and spirit. A generous neighbor donated an old hot tub spa to me and it has been a blessing. We still go to Lake Powell or camping with friends as often as possible. I had to give up my driver's license, so I go with friends and neighbors when I can, and it has worked out fine. I no longer need a service dog, but her companionship is just as important as ever to me. She instantly runs to people seeking attention and giving her unconditional love in return.

During a period before I lived in Grayson House, I had discovered a family secret. My actual birth father had died in the Korean War and I had never been told about him or the circumstances of my birth. I was determined to learn more about the family I never knew. Within a year's time I had not only found several Air Force men that had served with my dad, but I had the chance to meet several folks who had grown up with him.

In 2009 I had the honor of flying to Arlington National Cemetery. A memorial headstone, with his name on it, was placed in the cemetery with full military honors.

I have written a soon to be published book detailing the lives of my dad and his best friend, who also died in the Korean War, and how my life was intertwined with theirs.

Overall, looking back at my life, it has been exciting and painful. I don't' believe I would have survived if it had not been for the canine companions Buzz and Pooh. Having a four-legged companion and friend is very important. It is part of our survival and we seem to be lost without them.

*"The great pleasure of a dog is that
you may make a fool of yourself with him
and not only will he not scold you,
but he will make a fool of himself too."*
~ 'Notebooks 1912' Samuel Butler

Thor: "A Gentle Giant"

*"Dogs are not our whole life, but
they make our lives whole"* ~ Roger Caras

rowing up as an army brat, Donna traveled with her family to faraway places like the Philippines, Germany, and Japan. This world traveling instilled in her a sense of adventure, and is probably why in 1958, she met (on a blind date), fell in love with, and married, Lucky Lovitt, a graduate of WEST POINT NAVAL ACADEMY. She married the love of her life, and they have been together for half a century. For nine and a half of those years they have been living in Prescott, Arizona.

During their 50 years together, Donna and Lucky have had five Great Danes, including *"Thor"*, a seven-year-old, 150 lb., black beauty, who is as sweet as he is large. Donna beamed, *"Thor is a people person, very friendly, certainly not a security system. He barks only when I leave him outside too long, he lets me know in no uncertain terms that he is ready to come back in the house."*

This behavior may be hard to believe when you consider that Great Danes, who are a very old breed (dating back to 36 BC) and are known as the *"Apollo of all Dogs,"* are able to bring down bears and wild boar. *"Great Danes are sweet, playful, and exceptionally affectionate,"* Donna said cheerfully. *"They love everyone and need to be around people. However,"* she cautioned, *"as puppies they need training to become well-behaved adults."* She then reminisced, *"Thor was eight weeks old when we got him, he loved to chew up my plants. He especially took a liking to my Monkey Pod coffee table with Juniper legs."* She then confessed, *"I can't bring myself to get rid of it because it has his teeth marks all over it".*

This is understandable when you consider that Thor has been diagnosed with Lymphoma of the colon almost a year ago. Unfortunately, the prognosis is not good. Donna sadly explained,

"The veterinarian said that life expectancy for this condition is usually about one year from the date of diagnosis, which would be a year in May." She continued optimistically, *"Thor is currently on Prednisone and he seems to be doing very well, it's as though he is in remission."* Then sighing she added, *"I am just enjoying the moment and savoring my time with him, while being realistic."*

Donna and Thor began visiting nursing homes when he was two, his good nature and gentle ways are a welcome to the residents. Even the most withdrawn will make an emotional contact with him, scratching his big ears (which he loves) and patting him on the head. Big Thor places his head on their hearts, both literally and figuratively. He loves all the residents, however he does have one favorite; a gentleman named Jim at Good Samaritan, who keeps a fresh supply of cookies on hand. A sure way to a dog's heart!

"Thor had to learn all the do's and don'ts of being in a nursing home, and he learned very well," Donna recalled. *"As large as he is, that's how big his heart is. Thor is very careful and seems to understand that the residents are somewhat fragile and must be handled with care,"* she explained. *"And, of course, I keep a close eye on him to be sure he doesn't step on anyone or lean against anyone, as that is a trait of Great Danes,"* she grinned, acknowledging his lumbering size. She then added, *"He also understands he cannot go into the dining room, so he will patiently wait at the door to greet the residents when they come out."*

"Thor is known for his many hats that he proudly models for everyone. Most dogs don't like hats, but Thor seems to love showing them off.

Thor's best friend, a seven-pound Yorky named *"Oscar,"* loves playing with him and doesn't seem at all intimidated by Thor's size. As Donna says, *"his size does not depict who he is."*

Sadly, due to his illness and the medication he takes, Donna has limited Thor's visits to the centers. However, they both continue to walk a quarter of a mile each day.

Donna shared with me about her love of wood carving. *"I belong to a group called 'Wood Bee Carvers of Prescott.' It gives me great pleasure to work with my hands. The type of carving I do is called 'relief.' I have made a carving of Thor's head and I am planning to create one more of him with wings, like the angel he is… and will be."*

Donna shared her thoughts about what is to come, *"I am just enjoying Thor as much as I can, while still preparing myself for his leaving. I think, as humans, our pain is compounded by the unconditional love they give us. I know I will not allow Thor to suffer; I will cradle him in my arms and stay by him as he goes to the Rainbow Bridge, where I know he will wait for me."*

"He is my other eyes that can see above the clouds,
my other ears that hear above the winds.
He is the part of me that can reach out into the sea.
He has told me a thousand times over that
I am his reason for being;
by the way he rests against my leg; by the way he
thumps his tail at my smallest smile, by the way
he shows his hurt when I leave without taking him.

"When I am wrong, he is delighted to forgive me.
When I am angry, he clowns to make me smile.
When I am happy, he is joy unbounded.
When I am a fool he ignores it.
When I succeed, he brags.
Without him, I am only another person.
With him, I am all-powerful.

"He is loyalty itself.
He has taught me the meaning of devotion.
With him, I know a secret comfort and a private peace.

"He has brought me understanding where before I was
ignorant. His head on my knee can heal my human hurts.
His presence by my side is protection against
my fears of dark and unknown things.

"He has promised to wait for me…whenever…wherever
—in case I need him. And I expect I will—as I always have.

"He is my dog." ~ Gene Hill

The Lady Who Accompanies the Dogs

*"No one appreciates the very special genius of your
conversation as the dog does"* ~Christopher Morley

P at and Don McNiven loved camping across the country with their children, daughter Keyen and son Scott. That's how they happened upon the city of Prescott. With a friendly climate, friendly people, and lots of potential activities, they knew it would be a great place to spend the rest of their lives. So, in 1988, when they retired, they traded in the severe winters of Hobo Junction, New York for the warm summer days of Prescott Arizona. Life was good for them in Prescott and they soon discovered that it was also a very *"dog friendly"* town. This was a great bonus, since they were big dog lovers themselves.

Pat said, *"We always had animals; dogs, cats, and even horses. Both of our children really enjoyed them, it was a really great time in our lives. I guess you could say it was an animal filled life."*

Sadly, Pat's husband Don passed away in 1998 of scleroderma, a connective tissue disease. Pat shared their experience, *"Don was on hospice care at home for the last nine months of his life. The people from hospice were amazing. I can't say enough good about them; they were just great."*

With her daughter Keyen now in Colorado and her son Scott in Africa, where he works for USAID, Pat keeps busy with her part time job at Jay's Bird Barn in Prescott. Pat said, *"I work two days a week and love it there. It is a nature loving store, we do not sell birds, but we sell everything needed for the backyard bird enthusiasts. Our customers are always happy, so that makes it a delightful place to work. I am a birder myself. Every Monday morning, a group of us ladies take our binoculars, go out and observe the birds in their natural habitat. We call ourselves the Monday Morning Early Birds."*

Of course, she also keeps busy with her Australian Cattle dogs, Ruby who is 2 and Sierra who is 3 years old. How do they get along? Pat said, *"They get along beautifully. At times they have discussions with each other; they are best friends, playing and sleeping together."*

Pat shared a funny story about Sierra, *"In the morning, when I am having my first cup of coffee, she jumps up on the couch and does a little somersault roll; it's obvious she is telling me to pay attention to her. When I first got Ruby, she was a little shy, so it took her a while to relax, but she is very comfortable now. Ruby loves to play catch, it's her favorite thing to do, she is a natural ball retriever. I take them both out to an open field to play, although Sierra is not in the least bit interested, she just lays on the grass, looking at us as if to say, 'what are you guys doing?'"*

"Since I've always had dogs, I guess you could say Ruby and Sierra are my 5th generation of dogs; however, this is the first time I have had therapy dogs. Ruby and Sierra have both trained with Andy Lloyd of Love Mutts and Dandy Dawgs. She is such a sweet and gentle trainer. The dogs just love her. Her method of training is so gentle and unique, and her knowledge just astounds me. I am currently taking her Canine Health class." Both dogs are now certified therapy dogs; Sierra for about one and a half years and Ruby for six months. I keep them busy visiting Good Samaritan Village, assisted care facilities, senior communities, adult care homes and hospice centers; a busy schedule for myself and the girls. Sierra loves people, she is very sweet, wagging her tail and handing out kisses, which they all seem to love. They both look forward to visiting the different places and are both great therapy dogs. *"It is so great to see the looks on the faces of all the residents when we visit,"* Pat shared with a tone of pride. *"They smile, and their eyes light up. They don't always recognize me, but they always recognize the dogs; I just happen to be the lady who accompanies the dogs,"* she laughs.

*"In order to really enjoy a dog,
one doesn't merely try to
train him to be semi human.
The point of it is to open oneself
to the possibility of becoming
partly a dog."*
~ Edward Hoagland

If I could be half the person my dog is,
I'd be twice the human I am.
~ Charles Yu

Shadow, the Miracle Dog

"Dogs love company. They place it first
in their short list of needs." ~ J.R. Ackerley

H ilde Riedel and Phyllis Cuseo had been friends since 1962, when Hilde left Germany for California, where she rented a room from Phyllis' mom. Hilde said, *"During the seven years I lived there, Phyllis and I formed a special bond becoming the sisters we never had."*

After she retired, Phyllis found heaven on the Colorado River in Arizona. She loved sharing her home with her many friends who came to ride sea-dos and play at the casinos. Speaking of Phyllis, Hilde chuckled, *"Video poker was her favorite game; her friends teased her about having a second job there. She was a bit of a river rat, and why not, she earned every bit of it."*

Knowing Phyllis had lost her two Yorkies (Yorkshire Terriers), a neighbor of Phyllis', who had a beautiful black poodle that needed a home, asked Phyllis to come see the eight-month-old puppy. As soon as Phyllis saw Shadow she fell in love with him, and he with her.

Phyllis loved her life in Arizona but missed her best friend. So, after Hilde had retired, Phyllis told her friend about an empty lot right across the street from her and suggested she buy it. Hilde jumped at the chance of being close to her best friend, and in 2006 Hilde left California for the fun and sun in Arizona.

Hilde became the proverbial aunt to Shadow. *"Whenever Phyllis went to the casinos,"* she explained. *"I told her to leave Shadow with me, so he wouldn't be lonely."* She then added, *"My home became his second home where he had his own bed, toys, food and lots of hugs and kisses."*

Hilde shared that, *"In January 2010, Phyllis planned a trip to California to help a friend that had just come home from the hospital. Usually we would have gone together, but I had a problem with my knee and I needed to take care of that first. I told her to go ahead and I would follow later. She understood and said this was fine, and added that she would take Shadow with her, as he loved riding in the car."*

On a beautiful clear sunny day in January, along the I40, a bright candle on earth was extinguished, and heaven welcomed a new angel. A witness explained to the police that the driver apparently lost control of her vehicle, crossed the center divider, hit the gravel and while trying to gain control of the car, it rolled. At that moment Shadow was thrown from the car, confused and scared he tried to run away; however, some kind strangers were able to catch him and drove him to a dog clinic in Barstow.

"The veterinarian told me that Shadow had a serious hernia and needed surgery," she recalled in a somber tone. *"I asked him to please wait until I could get there on Friday; it was Wednesday and I had to make arrangements to say goodbye to my friend of 45 years."* Remembering that painful and difficult time, she added, *"Thank God for my church family who stepped up to help me, because I was devastated."*

After the long lonely drive to pick up her friend's dog, Hilde recounted, *"When I got to the clinic in Barstow, I found Shadow in a cage, crouching in the corner. They said he had been nipping and wouldn't let anyone touch him. I opened the cage and the moment he saw me, he jumped into my arms and held me tight. As soon as I got him home, I immediately took him to see our veterinarian. The vet told me he couldn't repair the hernia because the muscle was so badly damaged. He then asked if I wanted to put Shadow down, I told him, 'Absolutely not! I will take him home and care for him.'"*

She then related what can only be described as amazing. *"The next morning the reverend and his wife from my church, came to the house,"* she recalled. *"And we did the only thing we could do; together we prayed over Shadow, asking for a miracle,"* she sighed. She then continued, *"Every week he got a little better, until the hernia was completely gone. I then took Shadow back to see our veterinarian. When he saw him, he asked me what I had done, and I told him we prayed for a miracle. He told me, we got one."*

Reflecting on their life together now, Hilde lamented, "After the accident, I never took Shadow back to his home across the street. Occasionally, I will catch him looking out the window, like he used to when Phyllis left him with me. He would hear the garage door open and know that his mom was home. I often wonder if he is still waiting for his beautiful white-haired mom to come home?

"I am so glad to have him," she said gratefully. *"He is as much a comfort to me as I am to him. We take walks in the morning and evening, and I just pray to God that I live long enough to care for him."*

Thinking lovingly of her friend, she pondered, *"I think if Phyllis could talk to us, she would tell us, 'You two will be okay, you just need to love each other.'"*

"Shadow truly is the miracle dog."

"We derive immeasurable good,
uncounted pleasures,
enormous security, and
many critical lessons
about life
by owning dogs."
~ Roger Caras

Sarge in Charge

*"If dogs could talk, it would take a lot
of the fun out of having one"* ~ Andy Rooney

When Tom and Lorean Michaels met it was love at first sight. Both were born on the East coast, Tom in Buffalo, New York and Lorean in Newport, Rhode Island. As fate would have it both moved to California where they met in 1987. Both were recently divorced, and both shared a lifetime love of dogs.

Tom said *"Before Lorean and I met, I had a huge Great Dane named 'Rinnie' and two young daughters who loved playing with him in our backyard. One day, my neighbor showed up at my front door and asked me if I knew that my 5-year-old daughter was walking around the block with Rinnie at her side. We lived on a very busy street, so I immediately ran outside just in time to see Rinnie walking up the block, herding my daughter, Andrea, pressing her to the inside of the sidewalk so she would not go into the street. I was ever so grateful that Rinnie had followed my daughter out of the yard that day and stayed with her the whole time. He surely saved her life."*

Tom shared another funny story about Rinnie. *"One night, while I was watching television, I heard a helicopter overhead, so I ran out back to see what was happening. The helicopter was shining its spotlight, and I could hear the police running from yard-to-yard. I got out there just in time to see one of the policemen looking over my fence and coming face-to-face with my 200 lb. Great Dane. I then heard the policeman yell out to the other officers, 'He definitely didn't come over this way guys.'"*

"This will always be my favorite funny story about Rinnie. But saving my daughter from what could have been a disaster makes me ever so grateful to him. Rinnie was a great dog and we were all brokenhearted when he left us too soon."

When they met, Lorean had a Cockapoo (typically a mixed breed between Cocker Spaniels and Poodles) named *"Cinnamon."* She informed Tom they came as a packaged deal, so luckily Tom and Cinnamon became best buds and then on September 3rd, 1988 Tom, Lorean, and Cinnamon tied the knot.

After Cinnamon passed away, they both missed the pitter-patter of paws around the house, so when they found a one-year old Yorky named *"Bandit,"* they decided to give him a home. The owners told them they gave him his name because he would steal all the toys from the other dogs and hide them away, so he didn't have to share them. Thank goodness he was an only child in the Michael's house, so no need to share.

Lorean said, *"Bandit was a great dog, we both loved him, and when he passed away, I really didn't want to get another dog because it was so heartbreaking."*

"However, soon after we started looking for another Yorky to rescue. We first searched online and contacted a Yorky rescue group in Illinois. We wanted to give a home to a dog that had special needs and would be harder to place. We were both working at the time and they seemed to think that was going to be a problem. We were disappointed, but didn't give up the search."

"Finally, we answered an ad we found online. The breeder had a one-year old male that she had bought to breed, but the dog wouldn't mate, and it was clear she did not want him."

When Tom picked up the dog that they called *"Sarge,"* he wrapped his legs around Tom and didn't want to let go. *"We now believe that he probably would have been euthanized if we had not taken him home."*

"I don't know who picked out whom that day, but we've had him for 7 years and he is the center of our lives. By the way, the breeder showed us why they named him 'Sarge.' She let Sarge out in the back

yard with a Rottweiler and Sarge proceeded to grab a toy out of the Rottweilers mouth and he got away with it."

Tom, Lorean, and Sarge left California in 2006 for the wide-open spaces of Arizona. Tom says, *"Sarge has warmed up to some of the other dogs in the neighborhood, but there are others he doesn't like, and he lets them know it."*

"When I take him for his morning walk, we almost always run into other neighbors walking their dogs. On one of those mornings, we were standing by the street engaged in conversation, and Sarge was furiously barking at all the other dogs. Our neighbor, Leah's dog, 'Spencer,' walked right up to Sarge and gently, but firmly, put his paw on Sarge's head as if to say, calm down little buddy. Ever since, he and Spencer have been the best of friends."

Recently, Tom and Lorean replaced their carpet with hardwood floors. Lorean said, *"Sarge has had a really tough time trying to get any traction. He'll start at the bedroom, head down the hallway to the kitchen, then slide around the corner in the living room. He has gotten a little better with it now, and he's also found a way to get even."*

"One of his favorite toys is a bone he carries around with him. He found out that if he drops it on the hardwood floors, it makes a loud noise. Now, if he feels he is being ignored he runs to get the bone and drops it next to us. He particularly loves doing it in the morning next to the bed." Tom chuckled, *"It's like he is saying, 'come on Dad, I need to go out!'"*

Tom and Lorean couldn't be happier with this bossy little guy, who is one lucky dog. However, it is obvious that Sarge is in charge.

*"No philosophers so thoroughly comprehend us
as do dogs and horses."* ~ Herman Mel

My Little Dog,
a Heartbeat at My Feet

"In the world which we know, among the different and
primitive geniuses that preside over the evolution of
the several species, there exists not one, excepting that
of the dog, that ever gave a thought to the presence of man."
~ Maurice Maeterlinck

W hen Sandra Anglin was diagnosed with congestive heart failure in March of 2009, she faced it with the same optimism that got her through Cancer as a teenager, Leukemia as an adult and most recently, the loss of her husband of 45 years, Terry in 2006.

While the prognosis was not good, she refused to allow it to consume her. She had her faithful assistance dog *"Sancha"* by her side to comfort her and give her the strength she would need, to face her future. Another thing that Sandy and Sancha shared was congestive heart failure. Ironically, Sancha was diagnosed with it a year earlier.

She shared the story about Sancha and how this little dog helped her and her husband through some very difficult times. *"In 1997, we fell in love with a little Chihuahua that one of my neighbors was selling. It was love at first sight for the three of us. We named her 'Dulce' and soon after adopting her, our family of little dogs grew to four. All of them were named after characters in 'Man of La Mancha', my husband's favorite play. Dulce was short for Dulcinea, Quio named for Don Quixote, Ali for Aldonza and finally Sancha, the baby."*

Sadly, Sandy's husband became very ill in 2005 and lost his battle with heart disease in 2006. For the last year he was homebound and the dogs were of great comfort to him, especially Dulce, with whom he had a special bond. Dulce would rarely leave his side, and was so heartbroken after he passed that she followed him soon after.

Sandy had her baby Sancha certified as an assistance dog, enabling her to be taken wherever Sandy went. So, she was never alone and got plenty of love from the little Chihuahua. This bond helped her cope with the depression and loneliness that often follows the loss of a loved one. Sandy explained, *"After 45 years of being together, it's as though a part of my body is missing. I keep busy with my church and friends that I've had for 40 plus years, but it just leaves a hole in your heart that is hard to fill."*

In late October, Sandy entered the hospital. She needed a triple bypass to save her life. She also had diabetes and only ten percent of her kidney function. The operation was a long shot to save her life, but she faced it with her usual positive attitude. Sandy decided, with her daughter Kim, that Kim would take care of the dogs while she was in the hospital; until Sandy was able to go home. Every time Kim visited, she would bring Sancha. It was fortunate that Sancha was an assistance dog, because she was able to visit and stay by Sandy's side for the entire day, even after surgery in ICU.

While she made it through the surgery, she has since been plagued with many other complications. She is now on dialysis and because of her diabetes has lost her right leg and left foot. She was moved to a rehabilitation center the day before Christmas where she is fighting with all her strength, she must be able to care for herself and her little Sancha. She even told her doctor *"I need to get better, so I can take care of my Sancha again."* Her daughter continues to bring Sancha when she visits, which lifts Sandy's spirits and puts a smile on her face.

Sandy is an amazing, courageous lady and I am very lucky to know her. You see, Sandy is not just a story to me, she is my older sister, my hero and someone of whom I have always been proud. It is the great hope of Sandy's family that her wonderful and faithful companion Sancha will continue to inspire her to fight on in her courageous battle.

UPDATE:

Unfortunately, Sandy lost her final battle and passed away 2010, just a month after the terrible tragedy of losing her daughter, Kim, in an auto accident. We, her family, believe that in her weakened state she just wasn't strong enough to deal with another loss. We will miss them both dearly.

"One reason a dog can be such a comfort
when you're feeling blue is that he
doesn't try to find out why."
~ Author Unknown

'Pepper:'
Margaret T. Morris Center's Greeter

*"The reason a dog has so many friends, is that he
wags his tail instead of his tongue."* ~ Author Unknown

Most dogs have one family, one home and a relatively small space to call their own, not so for Pepper. She is the resident dog at the Margaret T. Morris Center and the official greeter. In fact, I was greeted by Pepper when I arrived, and I immediately felt the sense of warmth in a home like setting. Kathy Cunningham, General Manager and Director of Nursing, has worked for the Center for three years and is directly responsible for Pepper's presence there.

"Pet Therapy was my favorite research project while getting my master's Degree," Kathy told me. *"When I was given the 'okay' to have a resident dog, I immediately set out to find the perfect dog for the Center, which is an Assisted Living Facility for Alzheimer and Dementia patients."*

Describing her search, Kathy recalled, *"I found an ad in the paper about an eight-year-old Australian Shepherd whose owners were going to be traveling. They knew their traveling would be too hard on their dog and it would be best for her to be with a new forever-family. However, they wanted to make sure they found the perfect home for her."*

"When I met Pepper I immediately fell in love with her," Kathy beamed. *"And I knew with her gentle nature she would be perfect as the resident therapy dog."*

Thinking back on the process, she added, *"Pepper's family interviewed several other interested families. However, after they visited the center, her owners knew she was meant to be here,"*

Kathy expressed with delight. *"Not only would she be happy here, but she would bring such great joy for the residents and employees as well. It would be a win/win situation for all."*

Pepper has now been at the Center for a year and half, and she is the bright spot in everyone's day. This is confirmed by all the smiles and warm greetings she receives as she moves among them. She responds cheerfully to the residents, yet her spirit is not the least bit deterred by those who might not be dog lovers. All the staff loves her, and there is always someone willing to take her outside to play or feed her at meal time.

"Pepper is free to wonder and visit residents and visitors," Kathy said happily. *"Except for the dining room, where she is not allowed but waits at the door for an ear rub and sometimes a snack that will find its way to her,"* She grinned.

"Pepper loves food and the residents love to feed her, so she is a little 'fluffy' right now," Kathy amused. Then quickly commenting, *"Dr Dow, the veterinarian who cares for Pepper, said she could stand to lose a few pounds, so we are working on keeping some control over her feeding habits."* She also added, "She does get some exercise when staff, residents, or visitors stop to throw one of her toys for her.

"Pepper really does love everyone here, although she does have some favorite residents who are all smiles and hugs when they see her. One resident, named Ethel, treats Pepper like she is her own dog, showering Pepper with affection daily. Another resident, Colleen, will search for Pepper behind her favorite chair or couch if she doesn't see her right away."

Watching the interaction of the residents with Pepper is heartwarming when we see their eyes light-up as she makes her way to each one we visit.

Kathy let me know that one of Pepper's favorite places is the *"Secret Garden,"* which is a beautiful therapeutic garden area created by a full-time plant therapist at the center.

As Kathy and I strolled through the garden with Pepper, I could feel my whole body just relaxing while the warmth of the sunshine peeked through the beautiful apple blossom trees in the garden. As we strolled, Kathy commented, *"Pepper was once found playing with a garden snake; she has a few cat friends in the area as well."* My guess is that Pepper loves everyone, big, small, human and animal alike.

Kathy said smiling, *"Pepper is just so caring and friendly, she especially loves greeting people at the door, and the guest seem to love it too. When she tires, and it's time for a nap, she can be found at another one of her favorite spots, behind a beautiful indoor theme tree that is decorated for each season and holiday."*

As we talked, Kathy walked me through one of the four neighborhoods in the center, Apple Blossom Way, where each resident has 13 neighbors, giving them the feeling of belonging to, and being part of, a small group of friends. All the residents share a dining room and activity area. In fact, we caught one of the residents taking an afternoon nap in a beautiful warm and tranquil setting.

While saying my goodbyes, I watched as John Proffer, the Activities Director, working with the residents in a small class like atmosphere. He spoke to them with a nurturing spirit, in a way we would want our own loved ones to be treated.

It is plain that the staff is dedicated to preserving dignity and individuality, while providing a safe environment. It's also clear that Pepper is dedicated to putting a smile on everyone's face... and she does.

*"If you can look at a dog and
not feel vicarious excitement
and affection,
you must be a cat."*
~ Author Unknown

Peggy's Little Buddy

"Dogs laugh, but they laugh with their tails" ~ Max Eastman

P eggy Pate said, *"'Buddy' was three years old when I rescued him from a truck driver who had to return to the road. I feel so lucky because he has always been such a good dog. He has a basket full of toys he loves, his favorite being his purple bear. He loves going for walks, so we go twice a day."*

"What about other dogs?" I asked. Looking at Buddy she smiled. *"He only tolerates them, probably because they're too fidgety."* Then adding, *"He is very sweet and prefers things to be calm."*

Peggy and her Buddy moved to CASA DE PINOS in Prescott, AZ a few months ago and they really love it, especially the beautiful view she enjoys from her living room window. *"In the summertime while the trees have all their leaves, I feel like I live in a tree house,"* she said enthusiastically. *"In the winter time, when the leaves disappear, I enjoy the beautiful view of Prescott."*

Peggy has had Buddy for a little over five years and says he has adjusted very well and is fine if they are together. When asked about his health, Peggy says, *"His health is good except that he has lost a lot of his teeth, but he does okay gumming his food."* Baths? She shakes her head, *"He just tolerates them."*

When asked about any funny stories, Peggy chuckled, *"Buddy loves to watch TV, or I should say 'commercials.' He knows which ones have dogs in them. His favorite commercial is the one where the dog says, 'Bacon! Bacon! Bacon!' He just goes wild when that one comes on. Another one he likes is the Carfax one. He just sits there in front of the TV watching until it's over and then returns to whatever he was doing."*

Peggy shared a story about her dad. *"My dad Charles got very ill and had to be moved to a nursing facility. His dog 'Tasha,' an eight-year-old Schnauzer was so distraught when he left that she passed away soon after, we think of a broken heart. Four days later my dad passed away. I like to think that Tasha went first so she could be there to greet my dad at Rainbow Bridge."*

Clearly Peggy and Buddy were meant for each other.

*"The dog is a gentleman;
I hope to go to his heaven,
not man's"*
~ Mark Twain
(to W.D. Howells, Apr 1899)

Jewell Family to the Rescue

"He is your friend, your partner, your defender, your dog.
You are his life, his love, his leader. He will be yours,
faithful and true, to the last beat of his heart. You owe it to
him to be worthy of such devotion." ~ Author Unknown

Sharon and Kent Jewell have spent almost half their lives together, and during the 50 years they have been married, they have shared their home with many four-legged friends. Most of them they got from rescue groups or from someone who knew they would happily open their home for any one of them.

Kent told me, *"The only dog we actually bought from a pet store was a Cocker Spaniel for our daughter, Michelle; she named him 'Muff'."* Reflecting back, he said, *"Living in Idaho for 25 years gave us the opportunity to enjoy fun and affordable camping vacations. Muff was a great camper aside from one problem, I would head out early in the morning to catch dinner and soon, here he would come, scaring the fish away. Dogs are like kids,"* he chuckled. *"They are always into something they shouldn't be."* Then with a sigh he lamented, *"Muff was with us until a heart attack took him."*

After Muff past away, the Jewells still had plenty of love to offer, and offer they did! Kent went on to share with me about a Cockapoo named, *"General"* that they took-in from a neighbor that could no longer care for him. There was also *"Bridgette"* and her litter of puppies who were abandoned by another neighbor. A rescue group found homes for all the puppies, while Bridgette stayed with the Jewells for the remainder of her life. However, that wasn't all. Kent then added, *"We rescued a white poodle from a few girls that found her in Mount Rainier, where someone had probably dumped her. Their landlord would not let them keep her, so we took her in and named her 'Nikki'."*

Sharon joined the conversation, saying, *"Nikki loved going on camping trips in the motor home filled with kids. Although we only had the one daughter, her friends loved camping with us."* Sharon then added pensively, *"When Nikki started having seizures I learned that poodles are more prone to them."* Offering more detail, she explained, *"Due to their elongated neck, they get bone spurs in their vertebrae that sets off the seizures."* Then remembering their time together, she added, *"She was such a good dog, you could take her anywhere, however she never stopped looking over her shoulder; afraid we would leave her, I suppose."* Nikki was with the Jewells for 17 years.

Then Kent and Sharon also rescued a dog from a girl carrying it with a rope around its neck, saying she intended to throw the dog in the river if no one wanted her. Now, getting a bit impassioned, Kent describe the scene, *"I grabbed the puppy and told her she had no business having a dog!"* It was very clear that this one was still hard for Ken to talk about.

"We named her 'Brandy' and she was the love of our lives," he said devotedly. *"We had her for 12 years, and it was too short. The older you get, the harder it is to lose them,"* he lamented. *"After we lost Brandy we said we shouldn't get anymore dogs, it's just too difficult."*

This sentiment, however, didn't last long. In 1996 when the Jewells moved to Carlsbad, CA they once again rescued another Cockapoo, this time a black and white one. It had been from 'Cause for Paws' rescue organization who had found her abandoned in east LA. They named her 'Toshi'. Sharon added, *"Whatever happened to her, it must have been horrific because, even after 14 years with them, she never really bonded."*

Sharing their home with rescue dogs seems to be an irresistible calling for the Jewells. Sharon went on to describe how they met their current furry friend, 'Patches'. *"We moved out here to Prescott in 2004, and while driving around one day, Kent insisted we find the animal shelter and just 'drive by' there. Right!"* she scoffed. *"That's when Kent found a little dog he wanted, a Lhasa/Shiatsu, who had been wondering in Oak Creek Canyon, had been mistreated, or was in one heck of a fight. He was full of burs and his fur was matted,"* she recalled. *"His right leg had to be surgically removed,"* she said sympathetically. *"When he saw us, his tail started wagging, and he came running. We both told them, 'pack his bags he is coming home with us,'* she chuckled. *She then remembered,* "When Patches first saw our kitty, he ran and hid under our bed, but after a few days, they became friends. This year will be three years that we've had him," she smiled.

"We moved into Las Fuentes Resort Village in June 2011, and we are so thankful to be living in a place where dogs and cats are welcomed. We have a beautiful dog park here, its fenced-in so Patches and other dogs can be off their leash so they can make friends with two legged and four legged neighbors alike.

"When I went for my physical this year, my doctor told me I was in great shape for my age," Kent announced proudly. *"And he told me that I should continue walking Patches."*

Reflecting on his journey with all the rescue animals they've brought into their home, Kent pondered. *"I suspect that our pets take the place of our children who have all left the nest. Just like our kids, who we would reward for one thing or another, we now reward our dog in similar ways. If Patches is good at the vets, Sharon and I buy him a stuffed toy and peanut butter cookie."*

It is clear Patches is the center of their lives, a real 'Jewell'!

"A good dog never dies,
he always stays,
he walks besides you
on crisp autumn days
when frost is on the fields
and winter's drawing near,
his head within our hand
in his old way."
~ Anonymous

'McGregor:' A Westie Terrier with the Luck of the Irish

"Scratch a dog and you'll find
a permanent job"~ Franklin P. Jones

Gene and Jane Richardson both lived in Denver, Colorado where they met through a mutual friend. Things must have gone well because they just celebrated 21 years of marriage. After years of living in Colorado, they grew tired of the cold and shoveling snow, so they decided to head to a warmer climate.

They had already visited Bullhead City, Arizona, and liked the idea of living in a smaller town. So, in 2004 they packed up their motor-home and headed farther West. They wanted the heat and they sure got it with Bullhead, as it was known to reach 130 degrees in the dead of summer. Although, Jane confessed that she had no idea at the time about the heavy winds. Locals in the area joke that the wind only blows twice a year in Bullhead City, once from the north and once from the south. Still, it was warm, and with the Colorado River running through the town, the Casino only 20 minutes away in Laughlin, NV, Bullhead City became the perfect home.

Jane shared with me about her and Gene's love of animals, and she told me the story of how she and Gene ended up rescuing a precious dog they named appropriately 'Stormy'.

"One rainy night in 1989," she began. *"This very drenched dog, looking like a terrier mix, showed up on our front doorstep. We didn't have a dog at that time, but we did have a cat. And not knowing how they would get along, we decided to make her a bed outside that was sheltered from the rain,"* Jane recalled.

"The next day, our neighbors, who had spotted her, thought we should call the animal shelter. Neither Gene nor I wanted to do that," she said adamantly, shaking her head slightly. *"So, we told them we would just take her in until we could find her a permanent home—not realizing then, of course, that she had already found her permanent home with us. And it was where she lived happily for the next 17 years of her life."* Then, looking somewhat poignant, she added, *"until she passed."*

Recalling another memorable rescue, Jane continued. *"In 1993 we adopted 'Kyle', a Westie Terrier, from a friend who worked for a Westie rescue group. Kyle was sweet but didn't like children, which meant it would be hard for him to be placed. Therefore, we decided to give him a home,"* she said cheerily.

"He was a great dog who was with us for 14 years, until he passed away," Gene added.

"In 2007 we adopted 'McGregor', an adult Westie Terrier that we found online," Jane smiled. *"McGregor had been in a shelter when the rescue group grabbed him up and put his story and picture on the widely used Petfinder Website,"* she explained. *"He was about one and a half years old when we got him, and we've now had him for four years."*

Speaking of his rescue/recovery, Jane became solemn as she began to detail his story. *"He had been severely abused, to the point that you wouldn't even recognize him from then to now. He was afraid of the leash, and if you tried to put it on him, he would cower,"* she said, in quiet amazement. *"He also has back and spine injuries, which have led us to believe that the leash must have been used as some form of punishment. He now finally enjoys going for walks,"* she said with some relief and gratification.

"He is afraid of other dogs," she observed. *"Even the little Chihuahua across the way scares him,"* Jane lightly scoffed. *"Although, he doesn't mind cats. In fact, he had a cat friend across the street named 'Buster' that he loved to play with,"* she recalled fondly.

"Whenever Buster would tire of McGregor, he would just swat him on the nose, as if to say, 'Okay, I'm done playing,' and McGregor would simply walk away."

With some sadness, Jane added, "Sadly, Buster passed away recently, so McGregor must find a new cat friend."

As for McGregor's place in the home, "He knows that the sun rises and sets on him around here," Jane laughed. "I still work, but Gene is home with him, so he is never alone."

Spoiled? She laughed again. "Gene fixes toast for him every morning. Sometimes he fixes him toast and eggs! Oh, and don't try to give him toast without butter, because he won't eat it," she mocked.

"His favorite toys are two balls, one red and one green. He used to have other toys, but he always managed to somehow swallow pieces of them, which would then make him sick. The balls are exactly alike, other than the color, but if you throw the red ball first, he will sit and wait for you to throw the green one; his favorite. I don't know how," Jane bemused with a shrug. "But he knows the difference."

"He only has a few bad habits," Gene offered. "He hates the doorbell, and when guest come; he will bark and bark, and no matter what you say," he noted with some concern. "He won't stop! Then he will run and retrieve one of his balls and try to persuade guest to play ball with him," Gene smiled.

Gene began reminiscing about their other dogs, 'Kyle' and 'Stormy'. "We were still living in Denver and one day, while I was outside doing some yard work, I realized Kyle and Stormy had wandered off. A couple walked by, and I asked if they had seen my dogs. They said 'no,' but that they would keep an eye out. Soon after, here they came with Kyle on a leash and Stormy just following right behind them. She was such a great dog," he sighed.

Bringing the conversation back to McGregor, Jane remarked, *"The heat gets so intense here, most of our neighbors have rock gardens, maybe a few trees, but no lawn. So, Gene decided to put in a little patch of artificial grass just for McGregor. That way neither one of us has to make the trip to the dog park in the heat. He also has a treat dish that he will do just about anything for. We use it to train him for anything we want to get him to do, even to go potty on his man-made grass."*

One thing Gene and Jane both agree about is that McGregor is a doll and they have spoiled him rotten.

Sounds to me like McGregor has a bit of the *"Luck of the Irish."*

*"When a dog barks at the moon, it is religion,
but when he barks at strangers, it is patriotism!"*
~ David Starr Jordan

Mary and Herb's "Annie"

*"If a dog will not come to you after having
looked you in the face, you should go home and
examine your conscience. "* ~ Woodrow Wilson

In 2005, Herb and Mary rescued a one-year old Bichon-Poodle mix named *"Annie"*. Speaking of Annie's life before being rescued, Mary shared with me that, *"Annie came with some physical problems due to being tied up for long periods of time, and also having been run over by a golf cart,"* she said astonished. *"She is very independent and, unlike most poodles who usually love to sit on your lap, she will only sit on your lap if you have food."*

Sometimes, because of their poor treatment with previous owners, rescue animals have emotional issues. So, I asked Mary if Annie had any other challenges. She thought for a moment and said, *"There are other dogs that live on our floor, and Annie is not very friendly toward them."* Then joking, she chuckled, *"I sometimes think she doesn't know she is a dog."* Then being more serious, she added, *"One bad habit she has is getting into the waste baskets, so we have to make sure they are on top of a stool or in the bathtub."*

I asked Mary about Annie's health in general and her tone became sullen. *"Being a senior at thirteen years old, Annie's health is failing,"* she fretted. *"And recently she was diagnosed with Cushing's Disease."* This is a rather serious disease of the pituitary gland, affecting the adrenal glands and sometimes causing tumors there. *"The veterinarian told us she may or may not have a malignant tumor,"* Mary said, anxiously. *"But even if she did, they probably would not give her chemotherapy due to her advanced age."*

When asked when Annie started displaying her symptoms, Mary reflected, *"It started about six months ago. Her tummy got hard and she drinks over a gallon of water every day. She also is hungry all the time,"* she said concerned. *"If I put a lot of food down for her, she would eat until she dropped."* Lamenting her sweet dog's condition, Mary went on to say, *"Annie has slept with us for many years, but due to her condition, she has to get up a lot during the night to use her potty pads. So, she only sleeps with us for about an hour every night. We miss her being next to us, and I think she does too."*

Mary told me the very romantic and heartwarming story about how she and Herb met 27 years ago, *"We were both married, and both attended the same church but different services. However, I did meet and got to know Herb's wife Joan, while attending meetings together at church. I never did meet Herb until much later after Joan had passed away. My husband John, and Herb's wife Joan passed away within 10 days of each other."*

Mary continued, *"John and I were married for 44 years when he passed away of cancer, and Herb's wife, Joan, also died from cancer after 39 years of marriage. After John passed away, Joan wrote me a sweet letter of sympathy, and I will always think she wanted Herb and I to be together because she knew he would be lost without her... as he was so spoiled rotten that he couldn't even get a drink of water on his own,"* she laughed.

I asked Herb if he wanted to defend himself, but he just smiled.

Mary explained, *"After a close friend of mine sent me a letter about Joan's passing, I decided to send Herb a letter. I told him I knew Joan and how much she meant to me. Soon we talked about me driving down for a visit to California, where he lived. I found out later how much he hated driving, even as a teenager. I did ask him to send me a picture, so I would know him when I saw him."* Herb laughed, *"yeah she wanted my picture, so she wouldn't kiss the bell boy."* Mary and Herb went on a total of six dates, dinners, and movies. Then, within one year of their spouses passing, they were married. Mary narrowed her eyes, saying, *"Yeah, there was some criticism about that. However, a good friend and neighbor told me once, that most people who have long, and happy marriages want to marry again and soon."* Herb then added with a smile, *"See, it worked for us."*

When Mary and Herb talked about where to live, she told him she did not want to live in California, but that she loved Arizona. They have now lived in Arizona for 25 years and one year ago, they moved to LAS FUENTES RESORT VILLAGE in Prescott. Here they have made some great friends, and they love the convenience of everything being so close. Especially enjoying the many things there is to do there. In fact, Mary, who started writing poems and short stories in High School, has now renewed her love of writing by taking classes offered at Las Fuentes.

Both Mary and Herb dread the day that Annie is no longer with them. Mary grew melancholy, *"We will miss her laying on her back with all fours reaching to the sky, that is scratch time."* With Annie's condition and age, they really aren't sure how much longer they have with her. Mary remarked, optimistically, *"The old tail still wags with joy when we arrive home from time out. In fact, it wags a lot, even when calling her name. She also tells us it's 'ice cream time' by parking herself in front of the refrigerator and whining.* Agonizing over the thought, Mary sighed, "I think when we lose Annie, we will check into fostering pets. At our age, we don't want the full responsibility."

UPDATE:

Sadly, Annie passed away on September 11, 2012 during surgery. Our hearts go out to Mary and Herb for their great loss.

*"God's finger touched him,
and he slept."*
~ Lord Alfred Tennyson

'Mandy!'
The Best Little Birthday Gift

"If you think a dog can't count, try putting three dog biscuits in your pocket and then giving him only two"~ Phil Pastoret

R ay Patterson loves to talk about the places where he and his wife, Pat, have traveled. Smiling proudly, he declared, *"We've driven as much as 400 miles in a day. We once drove 30 days, sightseeing across country, ending up in New York at a Yankee game."*

The Pattersons have lived in Mexico, California, Arizona, Arkansas, and then back to Arizona. It's obvious when listening to Ray recount their travels that he misses having the ability to drive long distances.

The Pattersons married when Ray was 36, and by that time he had already been diagnosed with Rheumatoid Arthritis; a debilitating disease. Even before his marriage, Ray had undergone multiple surgeries; a triple by-pass as well as a knee and hip replacement, all when he was in his 30's. It is now going on 18 years that he has been wheelchair bound because of this bone degenerating disease. Despite this health challenge, Ray stays positive and active.

They have now settled-down in a beautiful senior community in Bullhead city, Arizona, in a house they had completely remodeled to accommodate Ray's wheelchair. Ray said, *"Moving here was the best thing we ever did. We have made wonderful friends here who are always ready to lend a helping hand; we both just love it here."*

For his Birthday in 2006, he decided he wanted something very special. He beamed, *"I found it in the cutest and smartest little Shih tzu puppy you could ever imagine, I named her 'Mandy'."* Since then, she has become Ray's constant companion, finding her favorite spot right under his wheelchair.

Ray bragged about his grandson's dog, *"My grandson has a Shiatsu that looks a lot like Mandy, but that is where the comparison ends. My grandson's dog is very obedient; he sits and lies down on command. Mandy on the other hand has a mind of her own, no tricks here. But what she lacks in obedience, she makes up for in sweetness, there's not a mean bone in her little body."*

Rays' 92-year-old mom, Estelle loves visiting, and even refers to their place as home. Since she and Ray both enjoy a good poker game, you can find them at the clubhouse at least once a week, playing 'Texas Hold'em.' Pat gets them both down to the clubhouse, then usually she hangs out in the library, chatting with friends, spending a little down time, or reading a good book while waiting for the game to finish. She is one of God's angels.

Speaking of his wife, Ray noted, *"For all intents and purposes, we are together 24/7, and have been for what seems like forever. I'm surprised we still get along so well. We're just very compatible. I have been in this wheelchair 18 years, so it's important to have a system, you need one to survive. You can't get any closer than we are."*

"What's your system?" I asked, curious.

"Well..." he started. *"When Pat needs to getaway, she'll go visit her daughter in Las Vegas,"* he said, gesturing in the direction of Las Vegas. *"She once took a cruise with her daughter, and another time she went to England to visit her brother,"* he shared. He then added with a pleased look, *"The grandkids then come and help me out here,"* he smiled broadly.

"I feel confident knowing that, if anything happens to me, Pat will not be alone, she will have her daughters to lean on." This brought a soft smile of gratitude to his face.

Shifting back to the subject of Mandy, Pat chimed in with this story, "*Our neighbor Jack used to get up every Sunday morning and cook bacon and eggs; he would always make a few extra strips for Mandy. It got to the point that Mandy would know when it was Sunday, or maybe she just smelled the bacon cooking. She would start howling,*" Pat scoffed in astonishment. "*If I didn't open the door fast enough, she would jump up on the table to make sure I saw her. Then when I let her out, she would run through their picket fence and right into their house, where Jack would give Mandy her bacon,*" Pat chuckled. "*After Jack and Jane moved, Mandy would go outside every Sunday and howl at the house, waiting for her bacon. I guess,*" she sighed. "*She eventually realized they weren't coming back. It was really sad.*"

Pat continued, "*Mandy's favorite place is a pillow that sits on a chair by the window. It sits just high enough that she can peruse the entire neighborhood. She really doesn't like the Mail truck or UPS, and barks fiercely when she spots them. The funny thing is, she doesn't bark at the garbage truck at all. Maybe it's because she follows me out to the street when I put the bin out.*"

Ray chuckled, "*You know how most dogs love to ride in cars, not so for Mandy. If you say, 'go bye-bye,' she will run and hide in her bed or under my wheelchair.*"

Pat quickly added, "*Unless you tell her we're going to see the grandkids; she loves the grand-babies. I put her bed in the car and that is where she lays until we arrive at our destination.*"

Asking if Mandy has a favorite treat, Pat eagerly said, "*Mandy loves green beans.*" Then noticing the puzzled look on my face, she explained, "*I was once watching a dog show on television, and they suggested that, instead of giving a bone as a treat, give them a vegetable like, green beans.*"

I was truly surprised to hear this.

"So, every night I give her half a can of green beans and she loves it. However, she especially loves fresh ones."

The trials that Ray and Pat have been through are not written on their faces. What you do see is the love they have for each other. Their neighbors and friends often see Ray riding his scooter on his way to the clubhouse. He typically has a smile, a wise crack or a joke, depending on how well the poker game is going.

Pat's friends say she is always smiling and they have never heard her complain. Ray confided, *"Pat is definitely a caregiver, there are things I just can't do for myself and she is right there."*

It is expected that your spouse will be there when you need them. Pat does it so effortlessly and with true grace. And let's not forget little Mandy, the best little birthday present anyone could get.

UPDATE:

Ray passed away April, 2012, and his mom Estelle followed November 2013. I like to think they are both enjoying a good game of poker, something they both loved. As for Mandy she is 12 and moving a little slower, and I imagine she misses Ray and her favorite hiding place, under his wheelchair

"No one appreciates the very special genius of your conversation as the dog does" ~ Christopher Morley

Living and Loving Life with 'Mackey'

"Anybody who doesn't know what soap taste like has never washed a dog." ~ Franklin Jones

J ean Krietemeyer recalled a childhood memory from when she was seven years old and spending time with her grandparents in South Carolina. *"One of my grandpa's dogs, a German Shepherd named 'Jack', actually saved his life. While they were walking a new bull to the barn, it broke loose and charged my granddad, Jack immediately lunged at the bull, grabbing him under his neck and hanging on, keeping the bull distracted so my granddad could get away. Jack was definitely a hero that day."*

Fast-forward to the present, I asked Jean about her current wired hair terrier mix named *"Mackey."* Visibly eager to share, Jean started, *"I found Mackey when I was 73 and he was just 8 weeks old. The first 3 years, he was into everything, and I didn't have a childproof home,"* she scoffed. *"At times I thought one of us was going to have to go,"* Jean quipped. *"However, he has more than made up for those first years,"* she smiled.

This happy duo now lives at CASA DE PINOS, a beautiful senior living community in Prescott, Arizona. Jean boasted about how Mackey is like a therapy dog to some. *"I have a friend here who is disabled, and when she's not feeling well, she will call and ask me to bring over her 'therapy dog,'"* Jean grinned.

"She says that Mackey just makes her feel better. Then, she calls me when Mackey is ready to come home; she knows when this is because he stands by her front door waiting for me to pick him up. I think he has been very good for a lot of the people here," Jean said gratified.

Recently, Jean had her carpet replaced, and while the workers were moving the furniture, they uncovered an old rawhide bone.

"All that day he stood watching over that bone," she jibed. *"So it wouldn't get lost again,"* she quickly added.

"While I was fixing breakfast the next morning, Mackey sat there watching my every move. It finally dawned on me that he must have hidden the bone again, and couldn't remember where he put it. He ran to his basket rummaging through all the toys, then went to his bed and began digging under the blankets. To his (and my) delight, that's where he finally found it."

"Mackey sounds like a real character," I teased her.

A big smile slowly grew on her face, *"When he thinks I am not paying him enough attention, he will jump right up on my lap and stare into my face."*

Now, shaking her head slightly, *"In the evenings, he likes it to be just him and me. So, if anyone comes to visit, he becomes obnoxious if they stay too late."* Gesturing back and forth, she says, *"He runs to them, then runs to the door, all the while yapping, and keeps doing that until they leave."*

Jean concedes that Mackey is spoiled, but she justifies it with a giggle by saying that everyone there, residents and staff alike, all had a hand it in.

"All of Mackey's toys are his babies," she cautioned. *"He particularly likes the ones that squeak; he grabs them with his teeth and shakes them until they squeal,"* Jean laughed.

"I should probably throw some of them out because they are so old, but he would be so upset if I did that," she fretted.

Clearly, Jean and Mackey are living and loving a wonderful life together.

*"I think dogs are the most amazing creatures,
they give unconditional love. For me they are
the role model for being alive."* ~ Gilda Radner

"My fashion philosophy is, if you're not covered in dog hair, your life is empty." ~ Elayne Boosler

Lenny and the Girls

"Dogs are miracles with paws" ~ Susan Rainbow Kennedy

I n 1994, Al Lambert and his wife, Lenny Lue, found and moved into their dream home in Prescott Valley. Lenny said, *"I knew it was home the minute I saw it. I feel I have been here my whole life and nothing would make me happier then to spend the rest of my days right here."* Lenny and Al shared a wonderful life, full of love, laughs, tears of joy and the ability to be in the same room—not saying a word—but just knowing how much you're loved. Unfortunately, their plans of spending the golden years together were all taken away too soon. Al lost his battle with Leukemia and after 40+ years of their life together, Lenny was now alone, and she was devastated.

Some only dream of the kind of relationship Lenny described to me, *"He was everything to me, he was my soul mate and the love of my life, and the aloneness I felt, did get me down."*

Looking back on that time, Lenny recalled, *"In June of 2007, I spoke with Kathleen Dunbar who worked at the Yavapai Humane Society, she suggested I look into adopting a dog to keep me company. She told me about a Greyhound adopt-a-thon and suggested I go see them. She also told me that these dogs were amazing companions and great 'couch potatoes'."* Lenny chuckled, then shrugged. "I thought it couldn't hurt and maybe it will help fill the void in my life.

"When I showed up at the adopt-a-thon, I couldn't believe how many dogs there were," she said astonished. *"I walked around a while just looking, when my eye caught a greyhound that was beautiful—white with tan markings. A volunteer told me that her name was 'Holly' and that she was two years old. I went over to*

Holly, put my hand out and she immediately responded; she was very friendly and affectionate. I spent some time with her and could see that she was a complete sweetheart," Lenny beamed.

"I talked to one of the volunteers about her and then told her I would still like to go look around, just to be sure I chose the right one for me. The volunteer agreed, and off I went. Soon, I came upon a kind of sad looking—surely older—black Greyhound with her head down and appearing very shy," she explained.

"I approached her, and she slowly wandered over to me. As I sat down next to her, she laid her head on my lap, then looking up at me. I quickly realized, it was love at first sight for both of us," Lenny sighed.

"I was told her name was 'Bonnie' and that she was nine years old. I then found myself wondering if there was room in my home and heart for both girls. The answer came to me instantly, 'Absolutely!'"

Lenny continued, "I spoke with one of the adoption volunteers and asked if it was possible to adopt two of the dogs. She directed me to fill out the applications and that I would get a call from someone to set up a 'home visit'. I soon got the call and set up the appointment. They came and after completing the visit, they could see that I was providing a wonderful home for the dogs," Lenny boasted.

"Finally, Holly and Bonnie moved in, and it's been the three of us ever since. I don't know how I survived before they came into my life. My friends now refer to us as 'Lenny and the girls,'" she chuckled with an air of pride.

"Holly is four years old and she is my débutante. Bonnie is eleven and she, like me, is a senior citizen. Interestingly their birthdays fall on the same day, June 27, just 7 years apart, also they were brought to me and moved in on June 27," she amazed. "It's as though we were all meant to be together."

Smiling, she added, *"Both are real 'couch potatoes'; content to lie around most of the day, but they are never far from my heels. I think, like me, they are just glad not to be alone anymore."*

Lenny herself is certainly no 'couch potato,' she has her own radio show on KJZA at 89.5 on the FM dial.

When I asked her to tell me what she does on the show, she responded. *"I'm a local exploiter!"*

Seeing my amused but puzzled look, she continued, *"I like to exploit all the wonderful things there are about the Prescott area. I encourage people to vote when we have an election, I interview locals and different charities. For new residents, I like making them aware of the resources available in our fine city,"* she said, enthusiastically.

These wonderful companions are far more than just pets. When we bring them into our home and hearts, they are like family. Being responsible for another life can add new meaning to our own, and having to care for and provide a loving home can also help us remain active and healthy. We give them food, shelter, and love, and they offer far more in return. They teach us about unconditional love, affection, and friendship.

Lenny told me about a plaque on her kitchen wall that reads, *"Once I thought I was wrong, but I was mistaken."*

Smiling now, Lenny reminisced, *"Al always laughed when he read it. Seriously though, I feel Al's presence here all the time. I just hope he is proud of me and what I do."*

Personally, I have no doubt that Al is extremely proud of *"Lenny and the girls."*

Lenny shared a poem she wrote for her husband and it seems a fitting way to close this beautiful story.

BLUE EYED BABY

What bright blue eyes like summer sky
My knees go weak, I breathe a sigh
That just one look could thrill me so.
The same as forty years ago.
The best for last, this wish for me
That for one moment I might see
Myself, my love, but through your eyes
The only wish my mind denies
The proof is plain, shown day by day
That love lives on and so I say
Though blue eyes fade to gray a bit
I would not change one day of it.

~ Lenny Lambert

UPDATE:

Sadly, Lenny passed away on July 31, 2013 at the age of 74, in Prescott Valley. I'm sure she was welcomed home and is forever embracing Al, the love of her life.

Keeping a Vigil for Judy

"We long for an affection altogether ignorant of our faults.
Heaven has accorded this to us in the uncritical
canine attachment" ~ George Eliot

We often find ourselves asking the question; why do bad things happen to good people? This story is about one of those times, and one of those people.

Bob Newman met Judy in 1981, after her sister Connie, who worked with Bob, invited him to go out with them after work one evening. Bob had just gone through a divorce and kept himself busy working and raising his three children. Lucky for him he decided to go and meet Judy. One year later they married and have now loved each other for 29 years. Throughout their lives, Bob and Judy have shared their love of dogs, all of whom were rescued.

In 1983 Judy, at 28 years old, was diagnosed with breast cancer. After her mastectomy, while she was recovering, Bob thought that a puppy might comfort her. *"I heard about a puppy that someone dumped in a vacant housing development,"* he remembered. *"When I found out that the people who found her were taking her to a shelter, I decided to take her home. The part Shepherd/Golden mix we named 'Ginger', turned out to be one of the best dogs ever."*

By 2004, Bob and Judy rescued a Springer Spaniel named *"Homer T. Buckshot."* He was a hunting dog whose owner (tired of hunting), had no more use for him. Sadly, he was going to leave him at a shelter where his fate would be bleak. Once again, Bob and Judy opened their hearts, giving 'Buckshot' a loving home to spend the rest of his days before crossing that Rainbow Bridge.

After Buckshot passed away, they rescued two more dogs, *"Jack"*, a Jack Russell, and *"Heidi"*, a Terrier/Chihuahua/mix.

Bob had to admit, *"Jack was just a mess when we got him, he got into everything. He ate two remote controls and one day, while at work, I received a call from our alarm company advising me that our alarm had gone off. I rushed home and found Jack sitting in a pile of Kleenex tissue. Evidently, he had thrown the tissue into the air and set off the motion detector,"* he chuckled.

"At four years old he has calmed down a lot," he sighed with some relief. *"We have taken these guys everywhere with us, Sedona, Prescott, Show Low; they have all been great travelers."*

Bob and Judy lived in Lancaster, California until they both retired in June of 2009. They then moved into a small, quaint senior community in Bullhead City, AZ, where they have made good friends and neighbors. Judy has been active in the community, working tirelessly, volunteering as director of the BULLHEAD CITY MUSEUM, visiting patients at VALLEY VIEW HOSPITAL and the WE CARE CANCER CENTER.

Regarding Judy's diagnosis, Bob cannot believe or understand how this happened to his beautiful, loving wife. He said, *"I'm a smoker, she's never smoked. I eat junk food, she eats healthy. She goes to the gym 3-4 times a week for an hour, I don't. This should not have happened to her; it should have happened to me."*

In February Judy was suffering with severe back pain and was referred to a pain management clinic in town, where they administered an epidural. Soon after that, she was back in the hospital, where she was found to have a cerebral spine fluid leak. She was then airlifted to SUNRISE HOSPITAL in Las Vegas, where they operated on her spine to drain the fluid. While there, she also suffered a stroke on her left side. They also had to perform a tracheotomy as a precaution.

Watching Jack lying on the floor, right next to Bob as we talked, with Heidi lying some four feet away, who was not too excited about having a visitor. It was plain that she is grieving, and the only visitor that would make her tail wag, had been away for two months.

Bob confirmed, *"Even when Judy would be gone for a few hours, doing volunteer work, Heidi would stay behind the couch waiting for her to come home. Our poor little 'Scruff-muffin', as we call her, just doesn't know where her momma is, and why she is stuck here with me for two months."*

Their son David took pictures of Heidi to show Judy, who clearly formed the words, *"That's my baby."*

David suggested to his dad that they could sneak the dogs in. Bob told him, *"Heidi would be okay but Jack is much too excitable. I could just see him now, running and sliding on the tile floors."*

Although Judy had no children when she met Bob, she has cared for and loved his children like they were her own. *"David considers her to be his mom, and that's what he calls her,"* Bob smiled.

"It's funny, when they are out together, people will remark to Judy, how much her son looks like her," he chuckled.

Judy has now been transferred to KINGMAN REHABILITATION CENTER in Kingman, Arizona, only 30 minutes away from their home. That is a welcoming change as Bob has traveled to and from Las Vegas, racking up some 6000 miles of travel in the last two months.

Bob has also been able to bring Jack and Heidi to visit Judy. Even though she was in a great deal of pain, Judy was still able to put on a happy face for her babies, Heidi and Jack. And I'm sure they helped bring a smile as well.

Just so we understand what kind of person Judy is, Bob shared this story, *"Friends of ours, from Whittier, went with us to Disneyland. While there, we all decided to go on the flight simulator. Judy is afraid of heights, but being a good sport, she went anyway. She kept her eyes closed the entire time,"* he chuckled. *"Except for once when she opened them, and it was just as we were going over a cliff and she yelled, 'Oh sh*t!'"* Bob laughed.

"Being shocked, her friend, Georgia, told her, 'I have never heard you say a cuss word!' We all had a good laugh that day, even Judy."

One of their neighbors, Betsy Stevenson, said of Bob and Judy, *"They are both such good people, Judy has worked so hard caring for others, you can see this has really taken a toll on Bob too."*

While Bob keeps busy visiting Judy, caring for their kids (dogs) and dealing with insurance companies, information about Judy's condition and prognosis is his primary concern. *"Life is like a blur right now,"* Bob confessed. He adds that her rehabilitation is painful and slow, especially for someone as active as she is.

So, while Judy fights to find her way back home, Bob, Jack and Heidi keep *"A vigil for Judy."*

UPDATE:

Judy got out of rehab in August 2011. Soon after that, they ran a test and found the infection had destroyed the mitral valve in her heart. So, on August 18th she had open heart surgery. Judy finally went back home on September 9th.

Robert takes her to rehab three times a week and works with her at home. She is now able to walk with some assistance and a hemi walker.

Gaining her strength, she has walked from 35 ft. to 300 ft. and going even further every day.

Bob is just thankful to have Judy home, and so are their dogs; Jack and the little Heidi, who never leave her side.

Judy remains positive about her future and so does Bob, who said, "Is it any wonder the staff at the rehab center call her the 'miracle lady'?"

"My dear old dog, most constant of all friends."
~ William Croswell Doane

Julia's Precious

"A dog is one of the remaining reasons why some people can be persuaded to go for a walk." ~ O.A. Battista

A refined, gentle and soft-spoken woman is how I would describe Julia Klausner. She moved to HIGHGATE SENIOR LIVING nearly a year ago, and the reason for choosing this facility was simple; *"They let me bring my dog 'Precious' with me,"* she smiled contentedly. *"Ann Conley is the Executive Director here and a nice lady, and Andrea Bahl is the Assistant director; they take such good care of me, always making sure I eat well. I think we all gain weight here because the food is so good,"* she chuckles.

Julia's love of animals started as a youngster growing up in Virginia. *"When I was a child we always had cats and dogs. Well, mostly cats back then,"* she said, correcting herself. *"Our cat would have kittens, and we got to choose the one we wanted to keep, and then we found homes for the others."*

Julia lived most of her adult life in California. However, one-by-one her family relocated to Prescott, Arizona and she decided to follow them. Julia said, *"I absolutely love it here, it's a really great place to live."*

When asked how she found Precious, Julia recalled, *"I found her in an ad in the newspaper. I picked her out of a litter of Shih Tzu puppies. She was the runt, but so adorable and beautifully marked; one white ear and one black ear."* With sincerity she conceded, *"Precious changed my life for the better."*

The caregivers here encourage us to walk our dogs, which I did do occasionally. However, if we cannot, then they walk them for us." *Highgate has a grassy area where dogs and their people get to mingle."*

When I asked if there were any funny stories about Precious that she wanted to share, she chuckled, *"Precious was potty trained on a potty-pad before I got her, so sometimes she would go out for the walk then come back and use her potty-pad."*

Describing her personality, Julia boasted, *"Precious was so friendly, she would go right up to people, nudge their legs wanting them to play. She was just a little princess, she loved everyone, and everyone loved her."*

Julia remembered, *"She used to have a boyfriend before we moved here; a Maltese that she loved playing with. I had a friend in California that would come up to visit occasionally, and Precious just loved him, and he loved her back,"* she said smiling. *"Whenever he was here, she pretty much ignored me,"* she scoffed.

Looking a bit amazed, Julia said, *"Precious was so sensitive to how I felt. If I didn't feel good, she would look sad, but if I felt good, she was happy. But then there were times when she would look at me as though she was upset, like I had done something wrong, but I never knew what it was,"* she bemused. *"They are so much smarter than we think. I read somewhere that dogs have the mentality of a four-year-old child... a very smart four-year-old child,"* she laughed.

Unfortunately, Precious passed away in Nov of 2011 from congestive heart failure. Speaking lovingly, Julia recalled, *"She was only nine years old. I thought she was having a seizure, but it was a heart attack. I knew it was her time when I took her to the veterinarian's office. When she was dying, I whispered to her that she could come home with me in her astral body, or she could go to doggie heaven. After she passed I felt like she was still around me for a long time, but I now feel like she has moved on."*

That brought up the story about 'Rainbow Bridge'

THE RAINBOW BRIDGE

Just this side of heaven is a place called Rainbow Bridge. When an animal dies that has been especially close to someone here, that pet goes to Rainbow Bridge.

There are meadows and hills for all our special friends, so they can run and play together. There is plenty of food, water and sunshine, and our friends are warm and comfortable. All the animals who had been ill and old are now restored to health and vigor, those who were hurt or maimed are made whole and strong again, just as we remember them in our dreams of days and times gone by. The animals are happy and content, except for one small thing, they each miss someone very special to them, who had to be left behind.

They all run and play together, but the day comes when one suddenly stops and looks into the distance. His bright eyes are intent, his eager body quivers. Suddenly he begins to run from the group, flying over the green grass, his legs carrying him faster and faster.

You have been spotted, and when you and your special friend finally meet, you cling to each other in a joyous reunion, never to be parted again. The happy kisses rain upon your face, your hands again caress their beloved head and you look once more into the trusting eyes of your pet, so long gone from your life but never absent from your heart.

Then you cross Rainbow Bridge together.

~ Author Unknown

Julia said she took up painting after she moved to Highgate. *"They have a lot of activities going on here every day. One day I decided to go down and check out the painting class. Sharon Forte is my painting instructor and so great with me. She shows us several pictures we can choose from to paint. Of course, I usually chose the desert scenes. Sharon did help me with an oil painting I did of Precious. I guess that is my favorite."*

While Julia's constant companion may be gone, she will always be Julia's *Precious.*

*"No Matter how little money and
how few possessions you own,
having a dog makes you rich."*
~ Louis Sabin

Jack Mantie and
His Amazing Companions

"Properly trained, a man can be dog's best friend" ~ Corey Ford

J ack Mantie was born and raised in New Jersey during the depression era of the 1930's. He married at the ripe old age of 19 and (along with his family) remained in New Jersey for 15 years while working in advertising on Wall Street. Jack now resides in Chino Valley, Arizona on a small ranch that he shares with his four-legged companions.

His love for dogs started early on. Thinking back to where his love of dogs began, Jack remembers, *"I asked my great-grandmother for my own dog when I was five years old, so she bought me a sweet male Cocker Spaniel that I named 'Buffy.' Even though my mother was a consummate dog-lover, she was absolutely terrified of Buffy,"* he recalls. *"He would sit on the couch all day, growling at her, until my father came home and took him off the couch."*Continuing his reflection, Jack shared, *"The first dog I actually bought with my own money (pennies I saved while in Kindergarten), was a male Collie I named 'Bruce.'"*

In the 1960's, Jack and his family traded their home in New Jersey for the mountains of Colorado, near Aspen, an area where they had vacationed many times. Jack says, *"I got a job working in a grocery store, earning about a third of what my secretary had earned on Wall Street, but we were happy there, skiing almost every weekend. We also opened a pet grooming establishment, which turned into more of a pet store, as clients continually asked us to order products for them."*

During that time Jack became interested in showing Collies. He found a breathtaking Collie named *"Wendy"* he purchased along with one of her pups. *"Wendy loved the kids, even picking* up their dirty laundry they left strewn on the floor," he chuckles. Around the same time Jack bought another Collie named "Lisa," who had been the lead-dog of a sled team. *"My love for my dogs was so profound that I even gave up my prized '57 T-Bird for a bigger car, making it more comfortable for the dogs,"* he confesses.

When his 9-year-old daughter, Jennifer, wanted a dog of her own (inspired by her dad's love of dogs), Jack was happy to indulge her. *"I found her an adorable and playful Shiatsu puppy, she named 'Ping Pong,'* he recalled. "He loved to follow me around when I fed the horses in the morning," he delighted.

Life took a turn for Jack in the mid 90's when he and his wife divorced. *"I moved to Arizona where my parents lived,"* he shared. *"I left the Collies with my ex-wife, knowing they would be well taken care of. After a brief time, I moved to Las Vegas and while there I adopted a Maltese named "Maui" from a couple that had divorced. She was with me for many years, until she passed,"* he sighed. Then smiling he remembered, *"I also rescued a Schnauzer named "Scotty" from a lady that could no longer care for him."*

Then, sharing how life threw him another curve, Jack said, *"I soon returned to Arizona with Scotty, to care for my ailing sister, Betsy, until she passed away in 2001."*

Then in 2007, Jack suffered a stroke that the doctors confirmed was so deep in his brain, it's a miracle that he survived. Most people who have been through rehab have rarely said they loved it, but here was Jack, just happy to be alive.

Asking about his journey to recovery, Jack smiled. *"I loved working out in the gym,"* he touted. *"Even on the weekends, while most patients took time off. I wanted to get well and get home, and that was what drove me."* Jack had nothing but praise for the rehabilitation facility. *"The food was great, and the staff were wonderful,"* he said straightforwardly. *"While I cannot drive now, I am about 75% back to myself."*

When asked about how he keeps such a positive attitude, Jack grew thoughtful. *"I have not always been so positive,"* he confessed. *"The stroke was a wakeup call, and I now love life to the fullest."*

When Jack returned home he had a welcoming committee consisting of his six dogs; *"Annie"* his therapy dog, an 11-year-old Australian Shepherd, *"Wings"*, a 9-year-old Shiatsu, *"Wiz"*, a 3-year-old Shiatsu, *"Goldie"*, a 3-year-old Shiatsu, *"Rocky"*, a 15-week-old Shiatsu, and *"Copper"*, a 2-year-old Shiatsu. Jack also has 4 cats that he rescued. Jack confided, *"I don't think I can take on any more responsibility at this point, as I am not getting around as well as I used to."*

Discussing the difference between dogs and cats, he says, *"The cats are typical cats, they sit on the breakfast nook and howl until I feed them, which is three times a day. The dogs are more like, 'Well, if I eat okay, if not that's okay too.' Not at all demanding, and like me, just happy to be here."*

Jack's doctor suggested he join a gym or purchase gym equipment to continue his physical therapy. However, Jack prefers to get all the exercise he needs by riding one of the four horses he keeps on his ranch instead. Jack explained, *"My workout is every day, caring for all of them, and in turn they care for me. I probably would have been long gone if it wasn't for the love I get from them. My concern for them is that they are happy, healthy, with wonderful dispositions."*

When asked how he handles taking care all of them and the work it takes, Jack said, *"I have wonderful friends that help out with the feeding of the animals. I don't play golf, I don't sit in bars, this is what I spend my money on, my amazing companions."*

"I talk to him when I'm lonesome
and I'm sure he understands.
When he looks at me so attentively
and gently licks my hands;
then rubs his nose on my tailored clothes,
I never say a threat.
For the good Lord knows
I can buy more clothes,
but never a friend like that."
~ W Dayton Wedgefarth

"It's a Wonderful Life"

"We give dogs time we can spare, space we can spare,
and love we can spare. And in return, dogs give us their all.
It's the best deal man has ever made." ~ M. Facklam

B arbara's chance encounter with Robert Olson in 1957 was not as much by chance as it was maybe by design. Both lived in Evington, Illinois at the time they met. Robert was visiting his dentist when one of the nurses suggested he meet the girl in the dentist office down the hall. Robert was curious, so of course, he did. Then, not only did he change his dentist, three months later he married that same girl. They both combined their families of *"yours, mine,"* and then added *"ours."* However, let's not forget Robert's two German Shepherds added to this blended family.

Barbara shared their story, *"Robert was 20 years my senior, so when we married he decided to retire from the family business, take is savings, and spend the rest of our time enjoying our lives."*

They began their search to find the perfect place. Bob loved to golf so naturally he wanted a community with golf courses. One of the places they visited was Victoria, the capital of British Columbia, known for its beautiful gardens, lush greenery and Mediterranean-like climate.

"Although we were smitten with it," Barbara started. *"Some of the residents that we spoke to, suggested we spend a winter there before buying,"* she continued. *"Due to the amount of rain they get, we decided to continue our search, until we came upon a charming home atop a hill in beautiful Carmel, California,"* she said effusively. *"The house wasn't even finished yet, but we didn't care, we slept on the floor,"* speaking now, with a chuckle in her voice. *"This was the beginning of our 35 years of joy in Carmel,"* she said with a warm smile.

When asked about her love of animals, *"We always had dogs growing up, so I have always been a big dog person,"* she remembered. *"I had a very special dog of my own when I was growing up, a Collie named 'Michael.'"*

Continuing, she said, *"While I was away at camp one summer, Michael, who was just nine years old, suddenly passed away. I believe he died of a broken heart, and I was just sick about it,"* she lamented.

Barbara talked about finding her current companion, *"When I lost my Cockapoo, I had a hard time recovering,"* she admitted. *"So, after two years, I decided it was time to welcome another dog into my life. I called a local poodle rescue group, NorCal,"* she recalled. *"And I told them I wanted a small dog that didn't shed. They told me they had two named 'Sampson' and 'Delilah', so I decided to take both,"* she quipped with pride.

"'Deedee', as I call her, was about ten years old, a very sweet little mini poodle mix with a fluffy white coat. Unfortunately, Sampson did not work out," she said with some regret. *"He was very aggressive toward other dogs and that concerned me, so I had to take him back. I felt horrible about doing that, but luckily, they had another lady who was interested in him, so that was a relief,"* she sighed.

"Deedee blossomed after Sampson was gone, I think he may have intimidated her a bit. She's almost 12 years old now, and doing great," Barbara chirped. *"I also have a sweet natured cat I rescued named Pooka,"* she added.

When asked how Deedee and Pooka get along, Barbara snickered, *"they tolerate each other."*

When asked if she had any stand-out stories about Deedee, Barbara quickly responded. *"The first day Sampson and Deedee came to me, they were both chasing Pooka, sailing through the kitchen along the tile floor. That's when Deedee slipped right into the table leg and dislocated her back hip,"* she said wincing.

"*I immediately took her to the veterinarian, and he was able to put her back together. But, when it dislocated again, they decided to remove the ball joint, leaving her with just muscle,*" Barbara recalled unhappily. Then quickly describing with some reassurance, "*She looks a little funny when she sits, but operates just fine with a little limp.*"

"*Robert passed away in 1989; he was 81,*" she said with sadness. "*We were so happy together, he was the 'love of my life,' I doubt I could ever meet anyone who could fill his shoes,*" she sighed.

Barbara's daughter (also named Barbara), decided to take a tour one day of GRANITE GATE SENIOR LIVING and fell in love with it. She had wished on a star that her mom would also love it enough to move from Carmel, California to Prescott, Arizona. Luckily her wish came true, and her mom moved to GRANITE GATE in November of 2012.

"*I fell in love with Prescott as soon as I saw the town square*" Barbara said glowingly. "*The old courthouse, the green grass, shade trees, and all the little shops and restaurants that abound there,*" she gushed.

"*My daughter is a very special daughter, and I am so glad we are close,*" she said with a sparkle in her eyes. "*She took me to one of those little restaurants,* KENDALL'S FAMOUS BURGERS AND ICE CREAM *shop where you build your own delicious hamburger, and then, at the front of the store, there is the ice cream bar. Yummy!*" she cheered.

"*I am very happy living at* GRANITE GATE," she beamed. "*Happy to be close to family; enjoying every day. I love the view from my penthouse, the trees, the mountains, I wouldn't trade it for anything,*" she insisted joyously.

Sounds like Barbara, Deedee and Pooka have found themselves a wonderful life in Prescott!

This one is for you Pooka!

"No matter what you've done wrong,
always try to make it look like the dog did it."
~ Mike Stevens

Helping to Heal a Broken Heart

"We long for an affection altogether ignorant of our faults.
Heaven has accorded this to us in the
uncritical canine attachment" ~ George Eliot

More and more healthcare professionals are seeing how valuable pets are when dealing with illness or depression. Assisted care and hospice facilities are opening their wards to animal companions as therapy. Judith Siegel, a professor at UCLA's School of Health, who has a PHD in sociology psychology, tracked a study of 1000 senior citizen who were enrolled in an HMO. The researchers found that people who had animals sought out their doctor far less than those who didn't. The seniors are convinced that their health has improved by having a constant pet companion there, and if it truly works, who are we to argue with them. As my dear mother used to say, *"The proof is in the pudding."*

Barbara and her husband, Ron, had lived and worked in California where they raised their family. Like most people in their fifties, they were looking forward to retirement and spending a long life together. They had been able to put away a little nest egg, and with that, they purchased a new home in a beautiful 55+ community, nestled in the hills of Bullhead City, Arizona. They were excited to be able to plan what should have been, the best years of their life. Barbara told me that she and Ron were so close, in fact, that their friends would always say, *"When you saw one, you knew the other wasn't far behind."*

When we settled down to talk, one of Barbara's dogs jumped up on the big overstuffed chair where she sat and laid on Barbara's leg. Then, not to be outdone, the other did the same on the other side. There, they both lay quite content, while she scratched their ears.

Barbara began by telling me that in 2007 she and Ron, along with their dogs, *"Scooby"* (a white miniature poodle) and *"Rowdy"* (a brown Yorkshire Terrier), moved into the house that they had planned to retire in. Sadly, on June 12, 2007, Barbara's world and all her dreams came crashing down around her. Quite suddenly, after a short illness, Ron passed away. Barbara was completely devastated.

"I felt so lost without Ron, like a part of my body was missing," she said somberly. *"We had been together for 20 years, and he was the love of my life; he was my best friend."*

Reflecting on the impact on her family, she remembered, *"My sons, who were also grieving their loss, were there for me as much as they could be. I am so grateful that they are so attentive that they'll call or come by and check up on me,"* she gently smiled.

"After Ron had passed away, I continued to work for a while. But then I had to retire as my health was in jeopardy."

I asked her to tell me a little bit about her dogs, Scooby and Rowdy, and how and when she found them. A peaceful smile came over her face as she eagerly shared their story.

"My friends at work actually helped me find them," she said. *"We searched for them on the Internet, and I originally was going to just get Rowdy,"* she paused. *"But then, when I went to see her, I spied Scooby in a cage, she looked so timid and alone,"* Barbara sighed.

"I found out she had been living in that cage for 7 years," she grumbled with contempt. *"She had been used to breed one litter after another, but because of her age and health, the breeders were no longer able to breed her, so they were trying to get rid of her,"* she said, disgusted.

"I just couldn't stand to leave her behind, knowing full well that if no one took her, they would probably euthanize her."

So, Barbara rescued both dogs that day, and in return, they would unexpectedly return the favor.

Like many seniors, Barbara was battling her own health concerns as well. However, added to this was also the understandable depression that came from the loss of her husband.

"Now that I'm not working, Scooby and Rowdy are the reason I get up in the morning," she said, adoringly.

"I think they just know when I don't feel well," Barbara reflected. *"Sometimes I'll have a bad night, so I'll have trouble getting up in the morning, and Rowdy will usually get right in my face, especially if I sleep past the time I usually get up. She wants her breakfast! Scooby is a little subtler. She just kisses on me a lot,"* she smiled.

"Someone told me," Barbara recalled. *"That when you have two dogs and one passes away, it's a good idea to have the surviving dog lie with the dog that passed, so that it will understand what was happening, and hopefully not grieve as badly as it might. Scooby and Rowdy liked to lie on the bed and cuddle with Ron when he was sick, and they were there when Ron slipped away. I honestly believe they did understand what had happened."*

Barbara then told me how she almost lost Scooby a few weeks after Ron had passed.

"I told the veterinarian, 'please do something; I just don't think I can bear to cope with another loss right now,'" she implored him. *"Thank goodness, with medication and being careful about what she eats, she is now healthy and happy,"* she sighed in relief.

"I know that at some point I will lose one or the other—Scooby is nine and Rowdy is five—but I know I will never be without a dog (or two)," she vowed.

Looking at them now, resting on her lap, she amazed, *"It doesn't matter to them how bad I feel or if I just want to spend the day in bed with them, watching soaps. They don't care what I look like; they love me just as I am. I really don't know what I would do without them,"* she worried, petting them with love. *"When I have bad days (and I do have them), I just pick them up and hug them, and they don't mind if I cry all over them,"* Barbara's eyes began to well with tears. *"What have they meant to me?"* She asked rhetorically. *"In one word, <u>everything</u>!"*

On the topic of dating or the possibility of marrying again, Barbara shared, *"I know it may sound terrible, but at my age it's more important for me to have Scooby and Rowdy then to think about another relationship. I had such a great relationship with my husband; that it would be difficult for someone else to fill his shoes. For now, I think the three of us are just fine,"* she said as she gave both of them a reassuring squeeze.

"They are like my children," she added. *"I leave the television on when I go anywhere, and they sit on a chair in the computer room until I get back. Then, when I get back home, they wag their tails, jump up and down, and give me hugs & kisses,"* she grins.

"The past few years have been very difficult," Barbara reflects. *"But Scooby and Rowdy have made it bearable."*

Before I left Barbara's house, I was able to get a kiss from Rowdy and Scooby, I said my goodbyes and wished them all well. But it left me wondering, *"Why do we love them so much?"*

For me, I concluded, it's that *unconditional love* that only a pet can provide, and that makes us melt at their touch. They kiss our tears when we cry, they keep our secrets, they never betray us, and only they can truly heal a broken heart.

NOTE:

Sadly, senior pets are often overlooked because of their age. As seniors ourselves, what a great gift we can give by adopting a senior pet and give each other the love that we all need. Remember: helping them will be helping you too.

"Did you ever walk into a room and forget why
you walked in? I think that is how
dogs spend their lives."
~ Sue Murph

"You ask of my companions.
Hills, sir, and the sundown, and a dog
as large as myself that my father bought me.
They are better than human beings,
because they know, but do not tell."
~ Emily Dickinson

Good Mornin' Glory, did You See the Rain, Dear?

"If having a soul means being able to feel love, loyalty, and gratitude, then animals are better off than humans." ~ James Herriot

S ally Harris was born and raised in St Louis, Missouri, where she lived for most of her life, working and caring for her mother and father. When asked when her love for animals started, she replied, *"My love for animals started when I was old enough to realize that there were all kinds of creatures in this world."*

Sally has rescued many dogs, like *"Maggie"* who she saved from euthanasia, giving this sweet dog nine more wonderful years of life. Sally's first rescue from a breeder was *"Mattie,"* who was deaf, had been bred for puppies, and abused for ten years. Sally said, *"She was a gentle creature, with whom I learned to communicate, thanks to the information provided to me by* BEST FRIENDS ANIMAL SOCIETY.*"*

Having cared for and loved so many dogs, Sally is no stranger to the loss of a companion and the pain that comes with it. *"Every time I had lost a dog, I would always say the same thing, 'No more! Never again, it is too hard!' Then I remember what a good friend asked me once, 'If not you, then who?' It made me stop and think."*

After Sally's mom passed away in 2010 she decided to move to Arizona, to enjoy a milder climate. Sally remembered, *"Before I moved, I shared a home with my friend, Margaret. A friend of Margaret's had adopted a dog named 'Ellie' but soon after, she had injured her knee. Margaret and I immediately stepped in to care for Ellie, until the friend was healed. However, about a month later, Margaret's friend called to say that she could no longer keep Ellie, and* *she may have to have her euthanized. Well, after I picked Margaret up off the floor (figuratively not literally), I told her I would <u>love</u> to give sweet Ellie a home."* Luck or divine intervention?

Sally told me that there are two C's in dealing with adopting a dog. The first is 'Challenge'; that would be the behavioral problems that might be brought about by breeding or abuse. The second one is 'Consistency'; when you build a bond with them, they are consistent in their love for us. No matter what kind of day I have, no matter what I look like, I am met with a wagging tail, and unconditional love. They are loyal to the very definition of the word. I am so grateful to have Ellie and feel graced by her presence."

After living in Prescott for a year with her brother, Carl, Sally decided to move into Alta Vista Retirement Community; a residence where Ellie is also welcomed. Sally chuckled, *"I figured we would try it out for a year and see how things went. Well, it's been a year and we're still here, and thankful for a great place to live. I often tease people and tell them Ellie and I are investigating tents. However, Ellie would put up her own sign 'Up for adoption' as she loves our apartment with all the creature comforts and has no intention of ever camping. My brother Carl says that Ellie lives like a queen because she sleeps on my $7,500 bed. Well, let me tell you, she deserves to know that there are those humans who understand that all God's creatures are important, and should be treated with dignity and respect."*

The staff and residents of Alta Vista feel the same way about Ellie, they love the shy little ball of fur. In fact, the staff told Sally if she ever left she would have to leave Ellie there.

Sally told me that Ellie has a 48-hour rule. She explains, *"My niece Katie came to visit from California. Ellie played with Katie all day, however, after 48 hours she acted like Katie was a stranger. I'm thinking one of two things; she is afraid she'll be taken away, or she simply likes it with just her and me. It is so strange because it is almost exactly to the minute of 48 hours that she starts treating Katie like a stranger. It's as though she is saying, 'Okay it's been fun, but you are leaving soon right?'"*

Sally shares with me some of Ellie's habits. *"Everyday Ellie and I go to the mailbox (yes, even Sundays). Ellie doesn't understand that the mail man doesn't come on Sundays, so we walk there anyway. I open the mailbox, look at her in surprise and tell her, 'looks like nobody sent us anything today', then she turns, and we walk back; she is satisfied,"* Sally grins.

Sally reflected, *"Ellie went from no life, to having a great life here. I remember something special my dad used to say to me in the morning and now I say it to Ellie. 'Good mornin' glory, did you see the rain, Dear?'"*

*"All the darkness in the world
cannot extinguish the light
of a single candle"*
~ Saint Francis of Assisi

Cinders: "A Beacon in My Life"

"Labradors are lousy watchdogs. They usually bark
when there is a stranger about, but it is an expression of
unmitigated joy at the chance to meet somebody new,
not a warning." ~ Norman Strung

Maybe Tom Cameron knew what he was doing the day he insisted that he and his wife, Virginia, adopt another dog. This came right after they had just suffered the loss of their beautiful dog *"Kelsey."* Tom and Virginia met, fell in love, and in 1987 they married. They were excited about retiring and looking forward to spending the rest of their lives traveling the world. However, eighteen months after they married Tom became ill and was later diagnosed with prostate cancer, and with a prognosis of a year to eighteen months to live. Undeterred by this news, they did not let it alter their plans. They continued traveling to faraway places like Thailand, Fiji, China, Australia, and New Zealand, just to name a few. Speaking of her husband's resolve, Virginia told me, *"Tom was a fighter, and he would not let cancer beat him."*

In 1992, he and Virginia decided to plant their roots in Mexico, about 15 miles from Baja. Virginia shared her memories from that time, *"Tom built us a beautiful home, right by the ocean. We even signed a 35-year land lease. I remember wondering then if, perhaps, we were being too optimistic."* However, in 1999, when traveling across the border became just too difficult on Tom (with its 2 to 3 hour long wait), they decided to sell their home in Mexico and move to Arizona.

In Arizona they found a beautiful little community, where they enjoyed spending time with new-found friends and neighbors, and where they found the support they both would need. They still traveled, however a trip they made to Glasgow,

Scotland (Tom's hometown), was cut short when Tom became very ill. The news they got from the doctor was devastating. Now Tom was diagnosed with cancer of the bladder, and it had started to spread to his stomach.

Virginia recalled, "After the loss of our dog Kelsey in 2008, Tom insisted we get another dog right away. I was not so keen on it at first, but then gave-in, insisting we only rescue a dog at the shelter; no designer dogs for me.

"When we got to the shelter, there weren't very many dogs to choose from. We saw this little wire-haired black and gray puppy that was very odd shaped; long body with short legs and just very strange looking. We then spotted a small white poodle with a cute little face. When we asked about her, they told us there was a long waiting list, so we decided to check out the little black dog again, which just happened to be 'Pet of the Week.'

"They told us she was about 5 to 6 months old; part Terrier and maybe Dachshunds or Beagle. She warmed up to us right away and seemed very happy. We decided, odd shaped or not, we were taking her home with us. We named her 'Cinders' because of her black and gray coloring." You know, they say, sometimes things happen just the way they are supposed to. Unfortunately,

"Just two weeks after we got Cinders, Tom took a turn for the worst and had to be hospitalized—never to come back home again."

"In the beginning, I brought Cinders with me to the hospital, so Tom could see her. After Tom slipped into a coma, Cinders remained home in her crate, or at least that's where I would put her. I don't know how, but she always managed to escape the crate, and when I got home, I would find pillows chewed and stuffing everywhere. I just couldn't bring myself to get mad at her though, because she was so sensitive."

"One day when I got home from the hospital, I found her outside at the front door, waiting for me. I guess we should have named her 'Houdini!'" She laughed.

Sadly, in June of 2009, Tom lost his valiant fight with cancer, and Virginia was left to cope without the love of her life.

"Tom was never afraid," she said with pride. *"He always had a peacefulness about him. Cinders never slept on our bed before, but now with Tom gone, it is comforting to have her to snuggle-up with. She is a real companion,"* Virginia cooed.

"She's the reason I walk every day, even when I don't feel like it," she confessed. *"She gets me out of the house!"*

Virginia chuckled, *"One of her favorite things-to-do is ride in the golf cart with me around the neighborhood, visiting her friends, and going to the mail box. The first time I put her in the cart, she jumped out while we were moving and scared me to pieces. Luckily, she was more scared then hurt and has never done that again. We are doing okay; one day at a time."*

While Tom's passing has left a hole in Virginia's life and heart, it is just as plain to see the big part that Cinders plays in her life. That funny looking odd shaped little black and gray dog she now calls *"a beacon in my life."*

UPDATE:

Virginia and Cinders met a wonderful man named Jack Heitz through a close friend. Jack fell in love with Virginia and Cinders (who he has nicknamed 'Tinder') and in May 2011 they married and moved to Mesa, AZ. They are now looking forward to spending the holidays with their family and close friends.

*"Even the tiniest Poodle or Chihuahua
is still a wolf at heart."* ~ Dorothy Hinshaw

As Good as it Gets
at the Kings' House

*"To sit with a dog on a hillside on a glorious afternoon
is to be back in Eden, where doing nothing was
not boring—it was peace"* ~ Milan Kundera

J im King met his sweetheart, Sandy Darby, on a dating web
site in April of 2004. I asked them, *"Was it love at first sight?"*
Sandy laughed, *"At our age, we can't waste any time."* That's
why, just two months later, Jim moved to Visalia, California
and purchased a home. For them it was a package deal; Sandy
with her Dachshund *"Trinity,"* and Jim with his dog *"Sassy."*
In March of 2006, Sandy and Jim were married in Laughlin,
Nevada, and together they started their new journey in life.

Sandy has four children; three sons, all in law enforcement,
and a daughter who is studying physical therapy. Jim had one
daughter, Tiffany, who was born with Spina bifida. *"I am very
proud of Tiffany,"* Jim shared with some emotion. *"She was so
beautiful and smart. She went to College, drove a car, and did everything
her body would allow her to do, until she passed away at 38."* As
we talked, he told me that the anniversary of her birthday was
only a few days away. It's a pain no parent should go through.

With Memorial Day on the horizon, I asked Jim if he wouldn't
mind sharing with me a bit of his stories of being in the military.
"Well, I joined the military in 1969 after my brother was drafted," he
started. *"Three weeks after boot camp, I was on the aircraft carrier
USS Kearsarge, off the coast of Vietnam. I went on to Moffett Field
where I was in the VP Squadron for 12 years. Then on the USS Kiska;
an ammunition ship,"* he continued. *"After being on shore duty in
San Francisco for some time, the Navy was getting ready to send me to*

sea again, and that's when I decided it was time to retire," he affirmed.

"After 21 years, starting out as an E2, I retired as a Master Chief," he shared proudly. *"I was only 39 when I retired, and I needed to find a new career. It was difficult trying to get back into the main stream,"* he remembered. *"I landed a job as a corrections officer at Corcoran State Prison in California. This was where they house such people as Charlie Manson and Sirhan Sirhan,"* speaking now in a serious tone.

"After 18 years I retired," he reflected. *"Mostly because my lovely wife was diagnosed with severe Fibromyalgia, and was bed ridden for months,"* he said, now looking at Sandy.

But after just eight months into their marriage, it was Sandy who had made some sacrifices. *"I quit my job to care for Jim after he was in a serious motorcycle accident,"* she shared. *"With life threatening injuries to his head and body, I did a lot of praying to God that Jim would live through this,"* she conveyed fretfully. *"After spending six months in bed, my prayers were answered! Thank you God!"* She praised.

Regarding their pets, Jim said he had been devastated when they lost Sassy, at just eight years old. He also vowed to never go through the pain of losing a close pet like that again. So, when Sandy suggested they go to the mall where rescue groups were holding pet adoptions, he wasn't very interested. However, he joked that he reluctantly gave-in when he remembered that the See's candy shop there gave away free samples.

"The first dog we saw was an adorable Shih Tzu/Pomeranian mix named 'Tilly'," Sandy remembered. *"She just went crazy when she saw us, so 'I' was sold. However, Jim was not very convinced,"* she gibed. *"One of the volunteers there suggested that we should go to the animal shelter where there were many more dogs just waiting to be adopted. We did too,"* she added. *"But we couldn't find a match, so we headed home. Later, I asked Jim if we could go get Tilly? At first he*

said, 'no.' But 10 minutes later, he said 'okay, let's go get her!' Luckily, she was still there."

Switching gears, Sandy smiled broadly, "Funny story about Tilly; when we go to bed at night, we close the bedroom door, so the dogs are in the room with us," she started. "They have access to their doggy-doors that go out to the Arizona room, then there's another doggy-door that goes out to the backyard," she continued. "When Tilly thinks it's time for us to wake up, she repeatedly hits the spring door-stop, causing it to make a 'boing-boing' sound," Sandy giggled. "If we still don't pay them any attention, they both run in and out between the doggy doors and we hear, 'flap-flap, flap-flap,'" she said, gesturing with her hands. "Trinity will also make low grumbling sounds. It's not actually a bark; more like she is mumbling."

Well, that certainly makes a great alarm clock!

Sandy shared with me that she believes it was divine intervention that led them to retire in Arizona. She explained that every year they would visit Laughlin to celebrate their anniversary. Then once, just before one of their annual trips, Jim was flipping through AARP magazine and saw some interesting property right across the river from Laughlin on the Arizona side, in a 55+ Solstice Community.

Jim then described how it all unfolded. "On our last day of vacation, we decided to see one of their properties. The minute we walked in, we knew it was our home. Then in May of 2012 we moved to Bullhead City."

Sandy added, "We had no fear, it was like God was telling us this is where we are supposed to be now, and we could not be happier. The community is busy, residents are friendly, and it's like being on vacation every day. We are stress-free, just what we both needed, it is truly a blessing."

In closing, I asked them, "So, what's on the horizon for you two?"

They both smiled and chimed in unison, *"A Hawaiian Cruise!"*

Sounds like life is as good as it gets at the Kings' home.

Personal Note:

Thank you, Jim, for your time in the military, and to all our brave men and women who protect us every day.

UPDATE:

Sadly, both Tilly and Trinity have passed, which definitely leaves an empty space in the hearts of both Sandy and Jim. However, for now, they are making plans to do some long dreamed of traveling. Then, after all their traveling is done, they may once again find themselves yearning to hear the sounds of, "boing-boing" and "flap-flap."

"Dogs' lives are too short.
Their only fault, really."
~ Agnes Sligh Turnbull

An Angel of Mercy

"The dog without his master
is like a body without a soul" ~ Mary E. Wilkins

For Marlys Hastings, the love of animals started as a very young girl growing up on a farm, surrounded by all of God's creatures; dogs, cats, chickens and all. However, her greatest passion would be her love of dogs. *"They have always held a special place in my heart,"* Marlys told me.

Later, after marrying and having children, she would pass her great love of animals along to her family. At present Marlys and her husband, Edward, share their home with two dogs, *"Pappy"*, a Papillion Bischon and *"Dakota"*, a Dachshund/mix that they nicknamed *"Kota."*

Reflecting on her life as a dog owner, Marlys commented, *"Seems like as one dog lived-out their life, another would show up in need of a home."*

Lucky for us, Marlys' loving and caring nature extends to humans as well, being a nurse for almost 47 years. For seventeen of those years she was in Hospice care, and for 9 years now, she has been with HOSPICE FAMILY CARE in Prescott as a Per Diem/Admissions Nurse. Her job may not always be an easy one, yet with Marlys' caring nature, it is one to which she is extremely well suited.

As one of her co-workers put it, *"I cannot say enough about how wonderful and caring a nurse she is. People are always commenting about the amazing respect she shows when caring for the patients. She can even tell when patients are thinking about how they will die, and she is able to have that conversation with them, putting their mind at ease. The love, compassion, and tact with which this exceptional person does her job, is a sight to behold."*

The discussions she has with her patients are usually both emotional and spiritual. Some of them have pets, and they worry about who will care for them when they have gone. Marlys can interject her love and respect for animals, assuring them she, along with the help of her fellow nurses, will do everything they can to find a good home for their pet. *"We don't need another Kevorkian in this world,"* Marlys admonished. *"We can medicate our patients to ease their pain, while still leaving them able to communicate with their loved ones until they go on their way."*

When visiting a person in their home for admittance, Marlys says, *"I always make sure to greet their pet(s) first, putting the person and pet at ease. I am aware of how important that relationship is to both. When you visit a home, you can immediately tell if the pet is part of the family or just lives there."*

Recently she attended the care of a gentleman who was on his deathbed. *"While there, I noticed there was a big beautiful German Shepherd in the back yard, looking quite sad,"* Marlys remembered. *"I suggested to the family to let the dog in, so he can have closure and know that his master is moving on. At first, they refused, saying the dog was too excitable. So, I assured them that with my help, we could contain the dog if we needed to. To their amazement, the big dog quietly walked straight to his master, licked his hand, then hanging his head, slowly walked away; his master had already passed. It was one of the saddest things to see,"* she sighed.

Remembering when her own mother passed away, Marlys shared. *"Mom's dog had been holding vigil under her bed for eight days. When she finally passed, the dog walked out of her room, jumped up in her rocker, and that's where he remained."*

At another person's passing she attended two years ago, she said, *"The woman had three long haired Dachshunds that sat on her bed and wouldn't let anyone near her. After some coaxing, they realized I meant no harm and let me close to her. However, even after she passed, they would not leave her side; it was really sad."*

Marlys also told me that after she is with someone who has passed, and she returns home to her dogs, they will come up and lay their heads on her lap, staying there a while. She believes they really do understand what has happened, because any other time they just come up, greet her, and go back to whatever they were doing.

We continued talking about the many heartwarming stories of people who have lost their spouse, only to have their pets bring them together with another pet lover. Feeling a deep sense of gratitude, Marlys whispered, *"These dogs are amazing, wonderful spirits."*

So, what is next for this wonderful lady?

"Last year I joined the RED HAT LADIES *and I just love it,"* she beamed. *"We get together once a month and have a great time. The oldest member of the group is 93 years young and incredible!"* Marlys said effusively. *"They are just a great group of gals. I realized, I really needed this outlet."*

It was both an honor and delight to spend time with this true Angel of Mercy, who is bringing such needed comfort to both humans and animals alike!

"The question is not,
'Can they reason?'
Nor,
'Can they talk?'
But rather,
'Can they suffer?'"
~ Jeremy Bentham

A Therapy Dog
Named 'Jordon'

"The dog is the only creature on earth that
loves you more than he loves himself" ~ Josh Billings

S CIENCE DAILY reports that, *"Therapy dog refers to a dog trained to provide affection and comfort to people in hospitals, retirement homes, nursing homes, hospice, and any stressful situations such as disasters."*

The term *"therapy dog"* is often attributed to Elaine Smith, an American who worked as a registered nurse for a time in England. Smith noticed how positively patients responded to visits by a certain chaplain and his canine companion, a golden retriever. These visits not only lifted their spirits, it is believed it also helped to accelerate their recovery and shorten their healing time. So, upon returning to the United States in 1976, Smith started a program for training dogs to visit institutions.

We are hearing more and more about the effects that these cherished companions have on the sick or the elderly. Health professionals have taken notice of the effects as well. Not only that their patients are lifted out of sadness and depression, but a visit from one of these companions relieves stress and lowers their blood pressure as well.

Billie Carlson, a retired nurse from BANNER GOOD SAMARITAN MEDICAL CENTER since 2005, began thinking about having an assisted therapy dog, and it just so happened that QUAIL HAVEN RANCH in Buckeye Arizona was looking for a good home for a five-year-old beautiful yellow lab named *"Jordon."* Billie and her husband, Bob, fell in love with Jordon and welcomed her into their home in 2003.

Jordon has a résumé that would be impressive by anyone's standards. Obedience School PetSmart 2003, Good Citizenship Certificate PetSmart 2003, Banner Good Samaritan Certificate for Therapy Dog 2003, and trained and accepted into Animal Assisted Therapy (AAT) Program at Banner Good Samaritan Rehabilitation Institute 2003. Gee, looks better than mine!

One of Jordon's many experiences, (too many to list) consists of visiting female inmates at Adobe Mountains Correctional Facility in Maricopa County. Billie said, *"Jordon was loved by the girls, who looked forward to every visit. They received the unconditional love they had not received in their difficult lives."*

In 2004 Friends magazine, from Banner Health Foundation, had an article titled, *"Just no Bones About It,"* which pictured Jordon with an MS patient and an occupations therapist. She was called the gentle giant during her tenure in AAT. Most dogs wake up in the morning wagging their tails in anticipation of getting breakfast, playing ball, and then it's nap time. Not so for Jordon, yes, she wags her tail and gets her breakfast, but then it's off to work she goes."

In 2007 Jordon began visits to Las Fuentes, Willow Winds, and Stanley Care Home after Robin Christie at Granite Mountain Hospice welcomed Billie and Jordon with open arms. They also visit the sick and elderly in their homes. Billie explained, *"Jordon's job is to comfort them and make their days richer with her visit. She takes the focus off them and their ailments by putting it on the big, sweet, furry, yellow dog who loves everyone."*

Billie and Jordon are now going into their third year with Granite Mountain Hospice. In 2009, Billie contacted Dr. Andrew Smith, the principal and superintendent of Model Creek School. One of the successful areas that Therapy Dogs Inc. has been used is in children reading programs. Dr. Smith said 'yes' to an interview with Jordon, and she was happily accepted into the program. In this program, the children from K-3rd grade get to read to her on a weekly basis. The children seem to be thriving with this new program. Thus, Jordon has become an integral part of the school week.

School is out for now, but, Jordon is not forgotten. She receives letters from the children thanking her for all she does to help them. When Jordon runs into any of her students in town, she always has a wag and a lick for them.

"Seems like the only thing Jordon doesn't like to do is have her picture taken," Billie commented. *"After she went through training at Banner,"* she began to explain. *"She had been chosen to be one of their 'calendar girls.' When it came time for her to pose for her picture, she bolted out of the studio, down the hall and into the elevator. As is with most divas, it took a little coaching to get her to return to the studio and photo shoot, then she looked as if to say, 'I'm ready for my close-up, Mr. DeMille."*

Therapy dogs are truly angels. The simple ritual between the sick and elderly with a therapy dog has become an integral part of the day for many who may have become despondent, depressed or have just given up on life. Watch a senior's face go from a pained look to a smile in minutes, it transcends our comprehension but cannot be disputed. Let's just continue letting these four-legged miracles work their charm. They truly are angels.

UPDATE: Jordon's mom, Billie, sent me this update.

"We had a very sad day on March 11, Jordon lost use of all four legs and we had to call our Veterinarian to our home to see Jordon off. This is a very big loss for many people, she had more friends than the rest of us. She was wagging her tail to her last breath and I thought of 'Rainbow Bridge.' I know she is in a fun peaceful place and we will see each other again. I miss her jubilant greeting when I come home from work. My heart is broken. There will never be another girl like her. Regards, Billie

"Treat me kindly,
my beloved friend,
for no heart in all the world
is more grateful for kindness
than the loving heart of me."
—A Dog's Plea
~ Author Unknown

A Saucy Little Lady

*"For me a house or an apartment becomes a home when you
add one set of four legs, a happy tail and that indescribable
measure of love that we call a dog,"* ~ Roger Caras, ASPCA

When Thea Dorman was born, *"Rin Tin-Tin"* and the *"Phantom of the Opera"* (the original) opened in the movie theaters; the year was 1925. Thea lived most of her life in California until moving to Arizona in 2006, where she continues to reside.

The history of Thea and her love of the Pekingese dog breed goes back to 1982 when she had stopped to gas up her car before leaving town on a trip. The attendant at the gas station (obsolete now) asked if she wanted a dog. Apparently, someone had just abandoned her there. She told the attendant that she was leaving town and couldn't take a dog. Then suddenly she caught sight of the pup, and it was love at first sight. Thea reflected on this chance encounter, *"She was just a 'throwaway' but spent the rest of her life returning the favor. I named her 'Girl' and she was a great companion; a real sweetie for 14 years. I was just heartbroken when she died."*

That wasn't, however, the end of Thea's love affair with Pekingese. *"I had a friend who bred Pekingese,"* she shared. *"One day, one of her Pekingese had gotten out, and befriended a Maltese/ Chihuahua mix. Naturally, a few months later the result was that she now had an 8-week-old female puppy that needed a home. My friend knew that I had lost my little 'Girl', and she also knew how depressed I was about it. At first I said 'no', but when I saw her big brown eyes (that I am sure she got from the Chihuahua genes), I instantly fell in love with her. I named her 'Saucy', which it turns out is the perfect name for her because she is so spry and loves to play."*

Since 1997 Thea and Saucy have been inseparable, best friends, and companions. That is until a few months ago when Thea suddenly fell very ill. She was rushed to the hospital after she suffered a breathing problem. Once at the hospital, she went into a coma, leaving her completely helpless. The doctors diagnosed her with Walking Pneumonia.

"I was completely out of it," Thea remembers. *"Thank goodness for my very dear friends from church, Opal and Bill, who took Saucy in and cared for her for the next three weeks while I was recuperating,"* she voiced with a tone of gratitude. *"Saucy didn't eat for the first three days that I was gone,"* her face now showing concern. *"She finally started to eat on the fourth day, but she was just not her bubbly self. However, I think Saucy must have smelled my scent on my friends after they visited with me, and this let her know that I was 'okay'. It also told her that she needed to eat now, so that she would be 'okay',"* Thea emphasized.

"I finally left the hospital and went into a rehab facility," she continued. *"I let everyone know there that I desperately needed to get well, to get home as soon as possible, as my little Saucy was very traumatized by my absence, and I missed her as well."*

While Thea was recuperating in the hospital her niece, Gwen, went to Thea's home and noticed a large wet area on the carpet in her bedroom. Gwen called the insurance company and they showed up to access the situation. They discovered that mold had developed due to water damage. Thea shared that she thinks this may have been what caused her illness to accelerate so quickly and severely. When she was to be released, she couldn't go back to her home until all the mold was removed and the carpet replaced.

"A good neighbor and dear friend, Lila Jo (who herself had no pets), welcomed me and Saucy into her home with open arms," Thea said with appreciation. *"We stayed there for three weeks, but I was still*

unable to take Saucy for a walk," she lamented. "So, while I was working to get my strength back, some of my dear neighbors came to take Saucy for a walk each day. Saucy didn't always go willingly," Thea scoffed. "But she went as far as she needed to do her things, and then get back to the house. I think she was afraid I would leave her again," she slowly shook her head.

"Saucy is my reason for getting my strength back," Thea boasted. "She encourages me to get better. We are finally back in our own home now and I am feeling stronger. We go out to walk at 5:30 in the morning, while it's still cool. When I grab for her leash, she dances around my feet playing the 'Catch me if you can game', which she loves. She is so good, and always listens to me," she delighted.

I asked Thea if Saucy had any challenges. "If she has any faults, I guess it would be food; she loves food," she stressed. "And everyone who loves her, also loves to feed her goodies." I could see that this concerned her. "We are working to keep her weight down to 12 lbs., and we are doing pretty good," she encouraged.

Concluding, Thea said with gratitude, "I am just so very grateful to everyone who stepped up and helped us through this difficult time. We are very blessed."

UPDATE:

Thea lived long enough to see Saucy off to the 'Rainbow Bridge,' and sadly, she has since passed away also. I am sure she is enjoying time with her Saucy girl again.

*"Having a dog will bless you with
many of the happiest days of your life,
and one of the worst."*
~ Author Unknown

A Man, his Dog, and
a Walk in the Park

*"With the exception of women, there is nothing on earth
so agreeable or necessary to the comfort of man as a dog"*
~ Phil Pastoret

Mary and Ed Goulette married in 1961 and spent their lives living in California. Mary worked for the 3M Company, while Ed owned his own Construction Company. Together they have had a long history with a certain Maltese named *"Maynard,"* and Mary shared with me a remarkable story about him.

"One night in 1995," she started. *"I had gone off to bed, leaving Ed in his recliner, where he would often fall asleep."* Then she explained, *"I had to get up every morning at 2 AM to be at work by 3 AM."* But this was not a typical morning. *"That morning around 1 AM, 'Maynard', jumped up on the bed and started scratching at my chest. I pushed him away, knowing I had only one more hour of sleep left,"* she said, seeming perplexed. *"He sprang back like a boomerang, this time removing the covers off my feet, nipping at my toes,"* she said in an astonished tone.

Something was obviously wrong. *"This time, I got up sprang out of bed, chasing him down the hallway, all the while thinking this dog has lost his mind. When I got to my husband's chair, I could see what Maynard was trying to tell me,"* Mary took a long breath. *"Ed was lying there on the floor. I immediately called 911,"* she quickly added.

"After hearing my story, the medics told me that Ed had suffered a stroke and that Maynard had most likely saved his life."

With Ed's health in jeopardy Mary decided, after 27 years working at 3M, to take an early retirement and move to Arizona;

to a small community and a slower pace of life. So, Mary, Ed, and their Maltese, Maynard, took off to the high desert.

Was it fate that Maynard was there? Maybe. Being curious, I asked her how she even found Maynard.

"I had gone to a breeder who was advertising Maltese puppies, when I saw this poor little dog in a cage, looking like a ragamuffin," she quipped. *"I couldn't believe he was eight months old, and from all appearances, had never been out of the cage,"* she grumbled. *"I went straight home and told Ed, 'You have got to see this dog, he is hardly recognizable as a Maltese, but there is just something about him.' Ed and I went back to see him, and the rest—as they say—is history."*

Speaking of favorites, Mary joked, *"There was no doubt whose dog he was; Maynard was by Ed's side, day and night. Ed had trained him to fetch his own leash, he would it put on him (as well as his favorite leather Harley hat), then off they would go to the dog park,"* she remembered.

"When Ed got too weak to walk to the park, he would ride our golf cart, with Maynard running alongside," she smiled. *"Sometimes, Ed would stop along the way, chatting with neighbors. However, if he stopped for too long, Maynard would use all of his 10-pounds to tug on the golf cart, as if to say, 'Come on Dad, the dog park awaits us!'"*

Sadly, Ed's health continued to diminish, making their daily adventure to the park difficult.

"When Ed became too weak to take Maynard on his walks," Mary continued. *"Our next-door neighbor, Elke Dickson, would walk him to the park every day, while I worked and cared for Ed. Elke had formed a real attachment to Maynard."*

Although, it was clear that Maynard was Ed's dog, whenever Mary would pull up into the driveway after work, he would be perched on the head rest of the recliner, just waiting for the front door to open. Mary would have to drop whatever she had in her hands to catch him as he leaped from the chair into the air, for fear he would break his spindly little legs. Mary told me that Maynard could be a bit of a hypochondriac too.

"One weekend, my brother and his wife, along with their German Shepherd, came for a visit," she began. *"In the morning, I was in the kitchen getting a cup of coffee when their dog came up and playfully jumped up on me. Maynard was close enough to see their dog jump up and come back down, but he was not anywhere close enough to get hurt. However, Maynard ran into where Ed was, and sat down with his paw sticking straight out as if to say, 'Look what that big dog did to me!' Ed insisted their dog had hurt Maynard, but I knew better,"* she grinned.

"The next day, while I was at work, I received a rather frantic call from Ed telling me I needed to get home and take Maynard to the vet because he was in pain. I picked him up and took him straight to the vet, where he stayed for two days. They wrapped his leg and gave me some tranquilizers to give him, telling me that Maynard really thinks he is hurt, however they couldn't really find anything wrong," Mary insisted.

"So, $800 later, I took him home and set him next to my husband, looked at him and said, 'Your Dog,'" she said with sarcasm. *"After we took off his bandages, I would look at him and ask him, 'How's your foot today?' He would start limping; only it was on the wrong foot, when I would tell him that, he would begin to limp on the other foot. It was an Oscar winning performance,"* she chuckled.

Unfortunately, Ed needed to go back into the hospital for a medical procedure, but while there he contracted MRSA (an antibiotic resistant staph infection). The disease literally wore him down from a 6' 4", 180 lb. man to a shell at 69 lbs.

Toward the end of his life, Hospice had come to the house to set up a hospital bed for him. *"Maynard did not like that hospital bed, the noise that it made frightened him,"* Mary recalled.

"One night he started tugging at the sheets on Ed's bed, so I picked him up and put him next to Ed, where he remained all night while Ed scratched his neck. Maynard knew his master was dying," she said solemnly. *"The next morning, Ed passed away."*

"Maynard went out to the scooter that was sitting lifelessly in the Arizona room, he jumped onto the scooter that he had never sat on and, staring at nothing, began howling. My neighbor Elke heard him and came over to take him and try to console him, but he was inconsolable," Mary sighed.

"Maynard was never the same after Ed died," she shrugged. *"I placed one of Ed's old shirts with him, hoping it would comfort him, but it didn't. He was seventeen years old but had always been full of life. Now he had become depressed; the light had gone out of his eyes, and the joy gone from his life."*

Sadly, Maynard followed his master in 2003.

These are both tremendously sad losses, to be sure; a loving spouse and a long cherished pet. Those who are left behind, do the best they can to cope with the loss of loved ones, and struggle to find ways to fill the emptiness with new life.

Thankfully for Mary, she found joy again in a little Shih Tzu puppy that a friend had given her on her birthday.

"He is a real show off who loves playing with all his toys," she gushed. *"One is a stuffed animal he treats like his 'Linus' blanket'. Whenever I have to wash it, he sits in the laundry room, waiting for it to finish. Then, when it's done washing, I tell him it has to go into the dryer. And so, he sits there, whimpering, waiting for it to dry. Another thing he loves is sitting on the patio table, watching the world go by."*

Although her job at the Colorado Belle keeps Mary busy, she takes time to relax on her days off; enjoying the little ball of fur she calls 'Nymph'.

"He gives my life a purpose," she confessed. "If I didn't have him, I probably wouldn't go out as much. He lets me know when he is ready to go to the dog park. If I am not careful," she smiled. "He sneaks out and heads to the dog park by himself!"

*"A dog can snap you out of
any kind of bad mood that you're in
faster than you can think of."*
~ Jill Abramson

A Promise to Keep

*"There is no faith which has never yet been broken,
except that of a truly faithful dog"* ~ Konrad Lorenz

Maryse Dunn came to America from France in 1990. She opened and operated a dog grooming business, but by 1993 she was missing her family and was ready to go back home to France. One day while Maryse was working at her shop, a gentleman came in with his Yorkshire puppy in tow. The gentlemen said he didn't know what to do about his dog's unruly hair. Maryse could clearly see the dog was in dire need of a professional grooming. The gentleman's name was Alton, and it was love at first sight for them both.

Their lives were forever changed, and aside from their love for each other, their love for their dogs would always be foremost in their life. Unsurprising, Maryse never returned to France. She chuckled, *"I would always remind him that he was the only reason I stayed here."*

They lived in San Diego until 2004 when they moved to make their home in Prescott Valley, Arizona. Maryse continued to work with dogs, grooming and training them for shows. Alton attended all the shows she participated in, even the confirmation shows that he wasn't particularly fond of. *"Al would tell me that he didn't need the judges to tell him his dogs were first class,"* Maryse remarked. *"He already knew that!"*

"Once, when one of our dogs took second place. He told me the judge didn't know what he was doing," she said, gratified.

Their dogs were their children, and truly lucky to be so loved by this couple.

"Like every couple, we didn't always agree on everything," Maryse said frankly. *"But we <u>always</u> had the love of dogs in our hearts. We could never have pictured our lives without them,"* she surmised.

Their wedding day also reflected their love of their dogs.

"Our children were away and not able to attend, so our dogs were our witnesses," Maryse giggled. *"Our Picard, Yorkshire, and Springer Spaniel were each dressed, wearing bow ties. Al and I thought it was perfect,"* she smiled broadly.

"One of our dogs 'Trinka', a Belgian Malinois—who was a puppy when we got her—has been the perfect dog; always ready to please," Maryse boasted. Then with concern in her voice, she shared, *"At one point we almost lost her; she had become paralyzed. I worked with her and was able to get her back on her feet. She is now eleven years old."*

Alton also has an extraordinary love of animals. Maryse shared a heartwarming story about his love of dogs.

"We were still living in San Diego and I was working at a Petco *there. I brought a rescue dog home, just for the weekend. She was a beautiful eight month old Border Collie mix who had spent the first few months of her life in a lab in Mexico. When I returned the dog after the weekend and got back home, Al asked me where the dog was, and I explained that I had returned her to* Petco,*"* she said matter-of-factly.

"Well, Al was visibly upset," she shared. He said to her *"We showed her what a good life was like, and then sent her back?' No!"* he insisted. *"You go get her and bring her back here,"* he demanded.

Maryse smiled broadly at me, saying *"Belle has now been with us for ten years."* Then pausing, and becoming a bit heartbroken, she added, *"She was Al's Favorite."*

As if a family of dogs wasn't enough, Al had discovered a parrot named *"Frankie"* who had been mistreated, and they adopted him without hesitation. Frankie was a year old when they found him, and he is now fourteen years old; safe and happy.

I asked Maryse whether she had any favorite stories to share about Al's love of animals.

She nodded 'yes' and said, *"About four years ago, when we lost our German Shepherd, Al was very upset,"* she recalled. *"He unceremoniously informed me that he was going to go to the animal shelter and get another dog. I had suggested he wait a while,"* she said, slowly shaking her head. *"But Al was the kind of person that when he wanted to do something, he was going to do it,"* she affirmed, slightly shrugging her shoulders.

"Later that day, he called me at work to tell me that he had adopted another dog," Maryse said, still shaking her head in disbelief. *"I asked him what kind of dog it was, and he said that he thought it was a Jack Russell terrier. Later he told me that he just took the first dog he saw from the door of the shelter. He didn't go in any further because he knew if he had, he would have brought them all home,"* Maryse grinned. *"That was Al."*

They also have a German Shepard named *"Seven"* that they got from a breeder. Maryse told me, *"Seven still thinks he's a puppy at four years old."*

Maryse and Al's love of dogs became their gifts to each other. Maryse bought Al a Springer Spaniel for his birthday and Al got Maryse a Berger Picard, for Christmas one year.

Maryse shared another story of one of Al's favorite pleasures.

"To my disapproval, Al loved feeding the dogs at the dinner table. All ten eyes would be staring at him. Al would ask, 'Why don't they go to you?' I told him 'Because I don't feed them!'"

"But, you know," she said pensively. *"It gave him great pleasure and that's all that matters."*

In February of 2009 Al was diagnosed with stage four cancer. He spent six weeks in ICU, during which time the chemotherapy treatments took a toll on his body, causing his kidneys to fail.

Of course, Maryse spent a great deal of time there with him and he would get upset and tell her, *"What are you doing here? You should be at home with our dogs; taking care of them and training Cyrano for the show!"* Maryse said, imitating Al's voice.

"Al was very proud of me as a trainer and always supported me in all that I did."

Ultimately, Al decided that all he really wanted, was to go home and be with Maryse and their dogs. His doctor, Dr. Campbell at Yavapai Medical Center, agreed.

"Al was so happy to be at home, with all of our dogs around him," she gently smiled. *"Al's Jack Russell, 'Jackson,' stayed by his side the entire time,"* she nodded.

Speaking of Al's hospice care, she noted, *"It was invaluable for all the help they gave us during that difficult period. I devoted all my time and all my love to Al and our dogs, making the last few weeks together beautiful, and I am so happy we did,"* she said, getting a bit choked-up.

"On Oct 24th and 25th there was a show at Fire and Ice Ranch, *we had both looked forward to being there. Cyrano, is going to be showing in the Herding Trial, as the first Berger Picard entered in an* AKC (American Kennel Club) *event. Al was very proud, and he made me promise that no matter what happened, I was to take Cyrano to the show, so they could see what a beautiful smart dog he is."*

Sadly, Al passed away at home on October 5, 2009, surrounded by their family of dogs and the love of his life, Maryse.

"Although it will be difficult," Maryse said, devastated. *"I will keep my promise to him; Cyrano and I will be there. I think Al will be watching as well, and I hope we will make him proud."*

While talking with Maryse, I could feel the tremendous sadness that overwhelmed her for losing the love of her life. However, just as clear, I knew that the many wonderful memories of the life and love they shared together will be the strength to get her through this difficult time.

"I know for sure one thing," she added with sorrow. *"And that is that I will need our dogs around me, now more than ever!"*

If the kindest souls were rewarded
with the longest lives,
dogs would outlive us all.
~ Author Unknown

*"People love dogs.
You can never go wrong
adding a dog to the story."*
~ Jim Butcher

Working Like a Dog

"The average dog is nicer than the average man"~ Andy Rooney

On June 20, 2009 we celebrated the 10-year anniversary of *"Bring Your Dog to Work Day,"* created in 1999 by Pet Sitters International to encourage the adoption of shelter pets. The event encourages employers to have their employees bring their dog to work for one day. I thought it would be a great idea to visit a few of these workplaces to see what (if any) affect this has had on the work environment.

Greg Krzmazick, Administrator at Prescott Valley Samaritan Center, brings his dog *"Mable"* (a four-year-old English Bulldog), to work with him. Although, Greg chuckled, *"She doesn't come in every day because she is such a couch potato."*

Another employee there, Tammy Cease, brings her dog *"Tyler"* (a four-year-old Australian Shepherd and therapy dog), to work with her every day. Tyler follows Tammy and visits with residents, where she gets plenty of hugs and smiles. We also heard that someone in the unit is feeding Tyler ice cream. I wonder who it is?

Betsy Gravel, is another employee there and also brings her three-year-old boxer *"Kisses"* to work every day.

"In the morning Tyler and Kisses will start playing, running down the hallway while the residents are having their breakfast," Betsy told me. *"And, while there may be a few that are not big dog lovers, Kisses and Tyler have been able to turn their hearts around,"* she beamed.

"Kisses likes to visit the therapy room where she can usually find a patient who will play catch with her. If a patient suffers with a weak upper-body, playing catch with Kisses is extremely physically beneficial for them, and they both enjoy themselves. I guess you could say it's a 'win-win' situation," she smiled.

Greg quickly added, *"Sometimes I'll be sitting at my desk, deep in work, and suddenly I hear Kisses give me a low growl, as if to say, 'Hello, there's a dog here. Where are my treats?'"*

Finally, I asked them, what affect (if any) has this had on either of them as employees?

Tammy immediately responded, *"I have been here for eleven years, and I am not going anywhere. Tyler and I are perfectly happy."*

Betsy and Kisses agree!

Next, I visited Joan Shay, the Executive Director of the ADULT CENTER OF PRESCOTT-COMMUNITY CENTER.

"My husband passed away last September," Joan began. *"And while 'Mitzi' [a gentle dog she rescued], allowed me to grieve for a few months, she began waking me up 2 to 3 times in the middle of the night, wanting to play,"* she said, a little frustrated.

"I eventually realized it was because she was home alone all day, with no one to play with. So, she would just sleep all day. That's when I decided to bring her in to work, to see how she would react" she said determined.

"Well, it's been three months now, and she stays active all day; visiting the workers, lying by the window, watching the world around her. Mitzi's favorite spot is to be on stage, however if she had her way, she would be in the MEALS ON WHEELS dining room," Joan grinned.

"I take Mitzi into the hall, before bingo starts, where she can interact with the visitors. They just love her, and she loves them right back."

I asked Joan, what affect (if any) Mitzi has had here in their office with co-workers and others?

Smiling gently, Joan said, *"I think Mitzi has made us kinder to one another. She seems to dispel any tension. The workers are clearly happier, and so is Mitzi,"* she added with a gentle smile.

"Sometimes, when they are intensely working, she'll walk over and nudge their computer mouse, to get their attention," Joan giggled.

"I think there's a misconception that dogs in the work force are disruptive. I say it's just the opposite," she stated emphatically. *"I would say it's like adding <u>dessert</u> to your day."*

It's interesting to note that the job search engine, SIMPLY HIRED, conducted a survey showing that one third of those polled said they would take a 5% cut in pay if they could bring their dog to work. Believe it or not... Wow!

Jeff Ian, owner of THINK4INC, said that for the past fifteen years, since day one, he and his employees have been bringing their dogs to work.

"My wife and I have always had 2-3 dogs, so it just made sense," Jeff explained. *"Our customers like it too. However, we do keep the dogs behind the counter and out of the customer area. Sometimes, when it's appropriate, if we have 3-4 dogs instead of the usual 6-7, we will let them run lose in the 6,000 sq. ft. warehouse in the back. But, for the most part they will lie close to us or under our desk."*

I saw that one of the dogs there, *"Skye,"* remained asleep on a blanket. Claire, her owner, told me that Skye is blind and almost completely deaf. When I reached to touch Skye, she immediately sprang to life, wagging her tail. How wonderful it is that Claire has seen past Skye's disabilities to become her ears and eyes.

When asked what affect this has had on his employees, Jeff said proudly, *"It makes for a comfortable environment. Our employees are like family, and they have been with us for many years. I can see no reason why these dogs should not be here with us".*

Jeff also shared with me that all their dogs are rescues.

I later discovered that Jeff also contributes a significant amount of printing to United Animal Friends, Search and Rescue, the Humane Society, as well as several other dog and cat non-profit organizations. Isn't it amazing what people will do when they have love in their hearts?

The American Pet Products Manufacturers Association estimates that 44 million households have a dog, and nearly one in five companies allow pets in the workplace.

I only have one question; what is wrong with the other four companies?

"I love a dog. He does nothing, for political reasons."
~ Will Rogers

'Baron Von Threetoes Jackson':
(The Happiest Dog in the World)
A Letter from an Alaskan Sled Dog

Hello there,

You don't know me, my name used to be "Threetoes." I'm a sled dog Huskie that was saved by a nice lady in Aniak, Alaska. That was a long time ago, and I will always appreciate the lady who saved and trained me, so I could get adopted.

Now, I am "Baron Von Threetoes Jackson," my pack is the "Jackson Pack" and I am happy to be a member. My pack leader's daddy, Tim Jackson, and mommy, Sharon Jackson, operated a hotdog truck in Anchorage, Alaska, and I loved it. I would get special treats every day—it might be reindeer sausage or buffalo hotdogs or just all beef hotdogs. These are just treats because my mom cooks for me every day and adds stuff to my kibbles. All this great food makes me very healthy.

We went to a park, four nights a week, and I got to meet a lot of people and other dogs. At the beginning I was very afraid, and kept throwing-up in the car, but mom let me sit on her lap until I got used to the car. Now, I go everywhere and don't get car-sick anymore. I was also afraid of a lot of things, like being inside the house and the noises around me. Now, I just enjoy it all, and I get to sleep with my pack in their bed, or climb into my own big soft bed.

I've learned a lot of things, like sitting, stay, come and speak. These are all important because I don't want to get hit by a car or hurt by someone. I still like to run every chance I get, so my pack leaders keep me on a leash when we take walks or go running in the park, where I have learned to retrieve my ball. I love, Love, LOVE, my ball!

In September, we went on a long adventure. We slept in a tent, and sometimes in a big motel. We traveled from Anchorage, Alaska to Bullhead City, Arizona. We went from being very cold to being very warm. My pack leaders say I am adjusting well, and I do now enjoy living in our new place. I have all kinds of room to run if I am on a leash. We go to the Rotary Park and I get to go swimming in the Colorado River and play fetch. The water is very cold, and it reminds me of Alaska, except it is warm when I get out of the water. I never got to swim before, so it is new to me. I am happy if I can play ball, because I love, Love, LOVE my ball.

There are some people in Bullhead City who want to build a dog park, (and they did). It is a great idea because there are so many dogs like me that want to be off the leash, getting to run and play with other dogs. The nicest thing is that I know I am loved. I get lots of hugs and lots of care. No one yells at me, and if I do get in trouble, it just gets very quiet and I have time to think about what I did. Luckily, I don't get in trouble much.

Most of my time is spent sleeping and just enjoying being a dog. Yes, I am a loving companion, but I am still a dog and my pack loves me for it. After all, they gave me a ball and you know how much they love, Love, LOVE my ball.

Sincerely,

~ Baron Von Threetoes Jackson

(The Happiest Dog in the World)

This letter was sent to me a few years ago, and the envelope it came in had been misplaced, so I am hoping that the folks who sent this to me to share will see it and know that Baron Von Threetoes Jackson has his day in print.

"A cat, after being scolded, goes about its business.
A dog slinks off into a corner and pretends
to be doing a serious self-appraisal."
~ Robert Brault

GUIDE DOGS OF THE DESERT:
"Creating Life-Changing Independence"

"All dogs can be guide dogs of a sort, leading us to places
we didn't even know we needed to go." ~ Caroline Knapp

T he word *"friend"* is defined in the dictionary as *"a person attached to another by affection or regard."* This has never been truer than the reciprocal relationship of a vision-impaired human and their guide dog. And this would also accurately describe Philip Weliky and his beautiful Golden Retriever guide dog named *"Avery."* This amazing dog has been with Philip for nearly four years and, in that time, Avery has given Philip a mobility and freedom he simply did not have before.

The AMERICAN FOUNDATION FOR THE BLIND estimates that every seven minutes someone in America will become blind or visually impaired. Only about two out of every one hundred blind people actually uses a guide dog. After learning this fact, I feel it is so important to share Philip and Avery's story and how the GUIDE DOGS OF THE DESERT has completely transformed Philip's life.

Founded in 1972 by Mr. Lafayette *"Bud"* Maynard, the dream for the GUIDE DOGS OF THE DESERT was finally realized with the generous help of the CATHEDRAL CITY LIONS CLUB. The new organization was finally incorporated and completely licensed under California State Law and the DEPARTMENT OF CONSUMER AFFAIRS.

So many humanitarian organizations have further donated to the GUIDE DOGS OF THE DESERT to assist in their growth and to bring much needed help to the blind.

In 1976 several members of Canyon Country Club in Palm Springs, California financed the purchase of property for the Guide Dogs of the Desert, and building renovations commenced.

In 1982, Lions Club members, local businesses, and a grant from the Lions Club International Foundation financed an expansion of the kennels and dormitory. Six more acres were also purchased for any future expansion.

By 1998, an additional kennel was completed, and this was made possible by the Mary Stuart Rogers Foundation. So many of these caring organizations are owed a tremendous debt of gratitude for their generosity.

Guide Dogs of the Deserts' mission statement is clear: "Guide Dogs of the Desert *improves the lives of the blind, creating opportunities for life-changing independence, and by conducting community outreach programs.*" As Philip said, "*This is a group made up of hard-working, selfless volunteers in a campus-type setting with a wonderful support system.*"

The potential guide dogs receive standard obedience training, as young as 6 to 8 weeks old, in a foster home. The most common breeds used as guide dogs are Golden Retrievers, Labrador Retrievers, and German Shepherds. These breeds are (more than not) especially smart, easy to train, and easy to care for. They are tested to see how they react to loud noises, or if they are easily distracted. These dogs are not trained by intimidation; they are trained to respond by love and hard work.

At about 15 to 18 months into the program, the dogs begin a more complex training. They build on the obedience training they have learned in a foster home with an instructor. However, now they must learn how to carefully navigate their human companion through traffic, across streets, into a subway, or up and down an escalator.

These amazing animals, with their remarkable skilled training, can provide what no one else can; sight for the vision impaired. If any of these dogs are just not *"guide dog material,"* they are gratefully returned to their foster home where they are welcomed and loved.

"I waited for about six months to get matched with a guide dog that fit my lifestyle," Phillip shared with me.

Once the match has been made, the blind companion is also trained at the school with his guide dog. And it was clear from the start that Philip needed to be matched with a guide dog that liked to walk, hike, and travel; by air, bus or anywhere a sighted person can go. As a service animal, Avery goes anywhere and everywhere that Philip goes, and he travels for free too! In fact, discrimination of a service animal is a violation of the DISABILITIES ACT law 101-336, enacted on July 26, 1990.

Philip and Avery's success story has become an inspiration to many others. They attend speaking engagements to share their story about the benefits of the human/animal bond and how this has liberated and enriched his life.

Besides being a member of GUIDE DOGS OF THE DESERT, Philip is also a member of the LIONS CLUB in Prescott. This organization recently donated funds needed to train a guide dog, who is appropriately named *"Prescott."*

I asked Philip if he could share with me a funny story about his experiences with Avery.

Nodding his head and with a grin he began, *"We had just de-boarded our flight, and Avery led me to the baggage carousel where he began sniffing each piece of luggage. Just then, a woman approached me and asked if Avery was a trained drug dog. I replied, 'No. Avery is my guide dog and he's helping me find my luggage,'"* Philip smiled.

"The women then asked, 'What does he do when he finds it?'

Suddenly, as if it was scripted, Avery yanked on the leash and began dragging me towards the carousel as I yelled out, 'this is what he does!'"

"Avery can maneuver well in several airports," Phillip boasted. *"Ontario, Long Beach, LAX and Orange County are just a few. Avery has no problem getting me to the ticket counter, elevator or escalator,"* he delighted.

"O'Hare airport was a challenge for me to maneuver through when I was sighted. Surprisingly, now with Avery I get there a lot quicker. Avery acts like a herding dog," he grinned. *"Weaving side to side, to find openings for us to get through."*

By the way, Philip and Avery were asked to appear New Year's Day on the Lions Club float, in the Pasadena Rose Parade.

To say I am humbled by this experience is an understatement. These guide dogs are heroic and loyal in their service and all they ask in return is a friendly pat and lots of love. Not a lot to ask for, in lieu of the enormous gift of freedom they provide.

If you want to volunteer, donate, or just want more information about Guide Dogs of the Desert, you can call them at 888-883-0022 or 760-329-6257 or go to their website at *www.guidedogsofthedesert.org.*

"Such short little lives our pets have to spend with us, and they spend most of it waiting for us to come home each day."
~ John Grogan (Author, Marley & Me)

The Emergence of 'Geena'

"Dogs don't rationalize. They don't hold anything against a person. They don't see the outside of a human but the inside of a human." ~ Cesar Millan (dog trainer)

The first time Marie and Dave Newman saw the honey colored Greyhound at a 'meet and greet,' they didn't understand why she was a quivering bundle of nerves, regardless they instantly fell in love with her.

The couple happily retired in a peaceful little town in Arizona called Prescott. They already owned an elderly, and mild-mannered, Greyhound named *"Jacques"*, but even his friendly presence seemingly did nothing to reassure her. *"Geena"* typically retreated into their deepest darkest closet, where she could barely be coaxed out for meals.

In those early weeks, Dave knelt on the floor for long periods of time holding out a dog biscuit, gently telling Geena she was a good girl, and that everything would be all right. Unless he moved away she would not approach him. If he made eye-contact, she would shake and shy away. They described it as being like trying to tame a wild animal.

When Marie and Dave searched the Internet for clues of Geena's pedigree, they learned her father had been a famous racer and several of her siblings had also raced, Geena herself had been raised on a training farm. Perhaps from the beginning the trainers realized she was not a racer and gave her up to the rescue group.

It was weeks before Geena began to timidly take treats from Dave's hand. She allowed David and Marie to take her on daily walks while leashed. It was several months before she felt secure enough to emerge occasionally from the closet, in search of human contact.

As time went on, she no longer trembled when she was with them, but she was still watchful and nearly always silent. However, she still would retreat to the closet when she felt threatened. It was her safe haven. When she heard someone at the door, she would shake and walk away, looking over her shoulder fearfully.

One afternoon last winter Geena began to bark frantically right next to the bed where Marie was taking a nap. Marie woke up suddenly and said, *"All right Geena, I'll let you out."*

When she walked around the bed toward the door, there lying down in a pool of blood was Dave. Marie knelt-down, calling Dave's name, but he didn't respond. She immediately called 911. The operator remained very calm, telling her to make sure the front door was unlocked and then for her to try to turn Dave over.

Marie managed to turn Dave's face to the side. The 911 dispatcher then asked her to check if he was breathing. It was hard to get her face down to his, but she was able to put her mouth to his and blew as strongly as she could; once, twice, three times.

She could hear the sirens approaching, and before she knew it, they were at the front door. Geena disappeared like a ghost in the closet. The EMTs performed CPR and intubated him; he was breathing.

Dave remained unconscious all the way to the hospital. Then, during the long, scary hours in the hospital waiting room, Marie was finally joined by her daughter, Donna. *"It was Geena's barking that woke me up"*, She told Donna.

Surprised, Donna remarked, *"Geena? She never barks!"*

"I know," Marie told her. *"She was barking like crazy, she knew something was wrong."*

Just then, the emergency room physician appeared with a clipboard in his hands.

"Dave is conscious and talking now," he said. *"We've been able to rule out stroke, and we'll be doing some other test to see whether he had a heart attack. By the way, what are the scratches on his arm?"*

"I didn't notice any scratches," Marie said with confusion. *"In any case,"* the doctor continued. *"They are superficial, and he is going to be okay. You can come talk to him now."*

Marie felt weak with relief. Her daughter handed her a tissue for her onslaught of tears. Only much later did they realize that the scratches on Dave's arm were made by Gena's paws, as she tried to turn him over, frantically barking for help.

*"The life spark in my eyes is
in no way different than the life spark
in the eyes of any other sentient being"*
~ Michael & Joanne Stepaniak

War Dogs. The Forgotten Soldier
by Dane Hays, US Army (Retired)

*What counts is not necessarily the size of the dog in the fight—
it's the size of the fight in the dog.* ~ Mark Twain

Throughout history military and law enforcement agencies have used dogs for a wide variety of jobs that were either deemed too dangerous or to help, aid, and protect his human partner from harm. Over the last 50 years, the U.S. military has used K9 service dogs (known as Military War Dogs, MWDs) to do many tasks that ultimately saved lives. To name just a few of these jobs: Guard/sentry duty, drug detection, and bomb/explosion search & detection. These dogs receive highly specialized intensive training and can communicate effectively with their handlers about a situation. They are extremely loyal, often refusing to leave an injured human despite being gravely injured themselves. MWDs can be aggressive and forceful on the job, yet docile and gentle with a baby at home, acting as though they have always lived as a house pet.

Many of us remember the 1946 movie *"Courage of Lassie"* with Elizabeth Taylor, in which a collie that had been used in World War I was owned by a young girl who faced public outcry over a possible *"dangerous dog."* Unfortunately, it was not until the Vietnam War ended that government attitudes towards MWDs began to receive some recognition and better treatment. Prior to that, when a dog was too old or injured, they would be euthanized. Now when a MWD is too old it can be retired, an injured dog will receive hospital/medical care, and those deemed able to adopt can be retired from duty and adopted by screened applicants.

Police K9s are often retired with honor to live out the remainder of their lives in the care of their handler/partner, sometimes receiving a care pension. Not so with Military War Dogs (despite congress approving a bill in 2008 for a National War Dog monument to be placed at Fort Belvoir, Virginia), no further recognition has been approved for these unsung heroes. In fact, in August 2008, the Pentagon refused a request from MWD handlers to honor our war dogs with an official medal for their service.

In Iraq or Afghanistan, an MWD saves a minimum of 3 to 5 soldiers per day or more. That alone equals approximately 27,000 soldiers a year that are able to come home alive from military service. Yet, these dogs receive no other official or public recognition for their service.

When they are injured, if possible, they can receive medical care and surgery. But sadly, those deemed too ill from either disease or injury are euthanized.

When the MWD is to be retired, the military puts the K9 through a series of tests. If the dogs fail any of the tests, he is unsuitable for adoption. Usually these are the dogs that have been trained in aggression or have injuries that could lead to aggressive tendencies. If the MWD *is* suitable for adoption, it is offered to the public through a carefully controlled program at Lackland Air Force Base in San Antonio, Texas. Sadly, there are no official medals, awards or recognition for their loyal service.

The UNITED STATES WAR DOGS ASSOCIATION, INC. is a non-profit organization of former and current US Military Dog Handlers committed to promoting the history of the MWD, establishing permanent War Dog memorials, and educating the public about these amazing canines. If you want more information you can go to their website at: www.uswardsogs.org

*Dogs have a way of finding
the people who need them.*
~ Thom Jones

*"The greatest fear dogs know
is the fear that you will not come back
when you go out the door without them."*
~ Stanley Coren

NOWZAD DOGS of Afghanistan
by Dane Hays

"Thorns may hurt you, men desert you,
sunlight turn to fog; but you're never friendless ever,
if you have a dog." ~ Douglas Malloch

Afghanistan is a country that has survived invasion, civil war, and religious wars during its long 3000-year history. Today, the country is once again torn between religious *and* political factions. To most of the Afghani people, dogs serve only two purposes in life; they are either the village scavengers cleaning up the garbage, or used for dog fighting. For a dog fight, the weaker dogs are maimed to make them more vulnerable and the fight usually ends in death.

In 2006, a British Royal Marine Commando named Pen Farthing, stationed in the Helmand Province at the forward operating base of Nowzad, Afghanistan, began a journey that would change his life forever. One morning he heard some loud yelling outside the Marine compound, the villagers had organized a dogfight. Pen broke-up the dogfight, not realizing at the time that one of those dogs would eventually adopt him. And over the course of his tour of duty, in one of the most dangerous places on earth, that dog would ultimately become his best friend.

Towards the end of his deployment, Pen realized he could not leave behind the dog he named 'Nowzad.' He knew he just had to take the dog back with him to England and the process was cumbersome and difficult. This process later motivated him to return to Afghanistan where he created a charitable organization known as NOWZAD DOGS, to help soldiers serving in Afghanistan with the process of taking home an Afghan dog or cat that had helped them deal with the stress & strain of combat duty.

Nowzad Dogs is not just the first, but the *only* veterinary clinic and animal rescue shelter in the nation of Afghanistan, located in the capital city of Kabul. Nowzad Dogs is a registered charity in the UK and a 501c3 (Free Non-Profit) charity organization in the USA. It has helped over 270 soldiers and their adopted animals by transporting the dogs and cats to the Nowzad shelter in Kabul, vaccinating and neutering them before arranging flights and transportation to the soldiers' homes in the west.

Nowzad Dogs relies totally on the kind donations of animal lovers everywhere to maintain their facility, cover the transportation, feeding, and medical care costs for the soldier's pets. Arrangements were made with specialists in the UK & USA to train and certify Afghan veterinarians. They also have a veterinary assistant training program for the local citizens. To date they have helped over 550 soldiers, from six NATO countries, reuniting them with the dog or cat that they could not bear to leave behind.

With over ten rescue requests from soldiers each week, Nowzad Dogs needs constant financial support. There are only two full-time administrators and the local support staff is either voluntary or citizens receiving a small salary of about $300 per month. Their goal, prior to the withdrawal of NATO forces in 2014, is to improve the welfare of the Afghanistan animals; humanely reducing the stray dog population; and provide animal welfare education (horses, dogs, cats and others) for the Afghan people.

Three trained Afghan Veterinarians are now on staff and several locals are employed in the care and feeding of the animals. Their aim is to re-home all the dogs coming into the shelter, first to actual homes in Afghanistan, and second to support soldiers and their adopted pets.

Because of the ongoing conflict around them, NOWZAD DOGS has had to relocate their entire facility twice in the last five years. Each move has required construction of fortress like walls because of the Taliban. They are now forced to move once again. This time they are building a state-of-the art veterinary/ shelter facility that will house over 100 dogs in kennels, a cattery, and a shelter for the ever-present armed security. This will be a legacy for animal welfare in Afghanistan.

Facts about NOWZAD DOGS: An approximate cost to rescue an animal from Afghanistan: for a dog is between $3500 and $4500 (more if it is an extra-large dog), depending on the currency exchange rates. A cat costs between $1800 and $2500.

The dogs get fed on a diet of 'soup' made from a mixture of meat stock, rice, na'an bread, potatoes, carrots and other vegetables, fresh meat, lentils and chick peas. Dry dog food is also added to the dog soup when they can afford to; the local cat/dog food is very expensive, however it is readily available. The shelter cats receive a diet of dry and canned cat food a couple of times a week.

What happens when an animal arrives at the shelter? Every animal receives a thorough health check and needed medical care by one of the veterinarians. All soldier or contractor rescue animals are micro-chipped on arrival and receive a rabies vaccination, as well as the first of a course of shots, to prevent other canine/feline diseases.

If you would like more information on NOWZAD DOGS, check out their website: www.nowzad.org

*"With some dogs, you share a boil-in-the-bag breakfast
and maybe a blanket on a cold desert floor.
But, if you're very, very lucky there will be
the one dog you would lay down your life for..."*
~ Will Barrow

The 'Star' in the Family

*"Without my dog, my wallet would be full,
my house would be clean, but my heart would be empty."*
~ Aplacetolovedogs.com

In 1998 Jack Hakim, along with his wife, Carol, retired and moved to Bullhead City, Arizona. It was a place, Jack said, they had been visiting since the 1980's. They purchased their home on the river in 1982, and Carol spent several years refurbishing and decorating. Visitors are greeted by warm, spacious and inviting surroundings as well as a beautiful view of the Colorado River.

When asking Jack about all the records that grace the walls in his family room, he delights in talking about where he came from and the life that he and Carol have shared for 45 wonderful years.

"Until coming to Bullhead City," Jack began. *"I had only one career in my life; that was the music industry. I had been involved with the marketing and production of two #1 records and three Top 10 records,"* he said with pride.

After moving to Chicago, he opened LONDON RECORDS, working with artist such as Jack Jones and Engelbert Humperdinck, to name a few. They then abandoned the cold weather too enjoy the sun and surf of California, where he worked for UNITED RECORDS. After a few years, Jack went to work for 20TH CENTURY FOX, and during that time, he and Carol were able to travel the world. Clearly these two had been enjoying a life that most people just dream about.

When they moved to Bullhead City, they loved spending time on the river jet skiing and entertaining. However, Jack, who never lets any grass grow under his feet, soon got bored.

So, he decided to become active in the local community. He went on to become a City Council member, then the Vice Mayor, and finally, in March of 2007, he ran for Mayor and won by a landslide.

Jack is proud of what he has been able to accomplish thus far. *"I proclaimed March 29th as 'Vietnam Veterans Day.' Havasu City, Kingman, and Parker have also introduced March 29 to the state and senate. Because we have done this, we can truly celebrate our Vietnam Veterans in a way that has not been done before".*

As a man who is not just a mayor, but a proud American, Jack also proclaimed September 13, 2010 as *"The Patriot Flag Day"* and World Memorial to honor the victims of September 11th, 2001 and the first-responders of the State of Arizona.

Gail Moscato, owner of Don Williams Jewelers in Bullhead City, and member of S.A.I.N.T., (SAVING ANIMALS IN NEED TOGETHER), was delighted to talk about Jack.

"I met Jack when he was a council member," she shared. *"I was impressed with his tremendous leadership qualities. I told him that he should run for mayor and that Bullhead City needed someone like him. I also know he loves animals, and I think he will make some positive changes for them. Change can happen in numbers,"* she said, encouragingly.

I asked Jack if he remembers Gail saying that and he said, *"Yes, I do remember her, and I remember her telling me that. She is a wonderful person, and I would love to find out more about her group."*

Jack has proven himself with his past to be a humanitarian, so his compassion for animals is a natural transition. He may be the mayor, but the *"real star"* in his home is a beautiful two-year-old fawn colored boxer named... you guessed it, *"Star."*

I asked Jack about his love for animals. *"Carol and I started off with cats,"* he replied. *"And then we rescued a number of dogs,"* he said looking at Carol.

"We rescued one in front of a grocery store," Carol added. *"Who turned out to be one of the best dogs we've had,"* she gushed. *"Her name was 'BJ'; she was a terrier mix, sweet, and very maternal."*

Carol continued, *"Once, while Jack and I were away on a trip to Europe, we hired a dog sitter for BJ and our poodle 'Cinder.' Unfortunately, a neighbor's dog got into our backyard, and because we had not spayed them yet, we came home to two pregnant dogs,"* she winced. *"When Cinder refused to nurse her pups, BJ took over nursing both litters."*

"We also had a German shepherd named 'Kemo'," Carol remembered. *"She passed away when she was thirteen; a long life for a German shepherd,"* she acknowledged.

Jack remembered another German shepherd they had. *"His name was 'Max'; the best dog in my life,"* he said effusively. *"We were inseparable; I could take him anywhere because he was so well behaved,"* Jack recalls. *"He was huge too, weighing in at about 150 lbs, yet so gentle with our grand-daughter, Juliette. When I took him out, people would always remark about how beautiful he was,"* he said fondly.

"He was also a 'search and rescue dog,'" Jack added. *"We both went for training, Max passed the training, but I failed,"* he said with a chuckle. *"They even asked if they could keep him there, and they would have someone else work with him. I told them 'No! That's my baby,'"* he quipped, shaking his head.

Sadly, they lost Max in 2006.

"I was devastated," Jack said, mournfully. *"There is not a day that goes by that I don't think about Max. I really didn't want another dog after he passed away,"* he sighed. *"But then there was Star, who was in dire need of a loving home."* He continued, *"We rescued her when she was six months old, and never having had a boxer, we had no idea what to expect,"* Jack gestured, raising his hands.

"At first, she was a little psycho," he snickered with a grin. *"But, with training and love, she has settled-in. She brings us great joy and happiness,"* his face now beaming with gratitude.

So, what is new and exciting in your lives, I asked?

Jack quickly answered. *"Our dog park is so important, and so needed for our community of dog lovers,"* he insisted.

"We have a hard working 'Dog Park Committee' that is diligently working toward our goal to complete the Dog Park," he noted. *"My hope is that the community will have a place to bring their dogs, where they can run free, meet some new friends, and just enjoy the beautiful weather here,"* he said, now gesturing to the sky around him.

Thanks to Jack and the Dog Park Committee, their dream was realized on July 28, 2012 when they had its leash cutting ceremony).

Sounds like Jack is not ready to retire any time soon and I believe the city and its animal population are glad about that.

UPDATE:

Jack and Carol lost their beautiful Star from cancer. They keep her ashes, pictures, and all the wonderful memories they have of their beautiful girl, who I am sure is now running and playing at Rainbow Bridge.

"If I had a pound [dollar],
for every time my dog
made me smile…
I'd be a millionaire."
~ Steph Harris

Learning to Heal
and Love Life again

"The greatest love is a mother's, then a dog,
then a sweetheart." ~ Polish Proverb"

S hell Palismo was a California girl who grew up *Hawaiian Style*, thanks to her dad Pete and her mom Marge. Pete was born and grew up in Hawaii, and although Shell's mom was a mainland girl, and Shell never learned how to dance the hula, play the ukulele, or speak fluent Hawaiian, they all embraced the Hawaiian culture.

Their home was always abuzz with a variety of *"God's little creatures"*; dogs, cats, even a parrot that Marge named *"Yenta."*

Pete had the biggest heart especially when it came to animals. He would go to the animal shelter and grab the first dog he saw when he walked-in, for fear if he went any further, he would bring them all home.

When Shell was little, she also rescued animals. She would find them, scoop them up, bring them home, and vowed to care for as well as love them forever. The animal rescue seed had already been planted, even though it would be years before she would fully realize it.

"My dad was only 17 when he enlisted in the Army Air Corp in Hawaii," Shell told me. *"And was there on that fateful day of December 7th, 1941,"* she added with a grimaced. *"He never spoke about it much, other than to tell me that because of his age, the Army wouldn't even issue him a hand gun."*

When Pete retired in 1966, he was told that the Army would not pay to relocate his family back to Hawaii, because he had retired in California. So, that is where they built their lives, yet his heart was always in Hawaii.

Sadly, it was a great loss when Shell's dad had a massive and fatal heart attack; he was only 49 years old, and Shell had just celebrated her eight birthday.

Together with her mom, Shell continued rescuing from shelters; a chocolate point Siamese cat named *"Ichiban"* and a kitten they called *"Sapphire,"* a pure white German Shepherd they named *"Susie,"* and a Chichi mix that they named *"Enchilada"* but nicknamed *"Enchi."*

"Enchi was round, like a bowling ball," Shell chuckled. *"But very smart,"* she added. *"You could hold your hand up with two or three fingers, and ask how many, and she would count out how many fingers you had up by pawing the glass on the back door. This was great entertainment for guest who came to our home,"* Shell smiled. *"The, 'how-many-at-the-backdoor' game was done over and over until she became bored and turned her back on us."*

Shell was 20 years old when she met and fell in love with Mike. Soon after they married and, with Mike in the armed services, they moved to the Philippines. This was Shell's first time away from her mom and family, so she was having a tough time adjusting to her new environment.

Knowing how alone Shell felt, Mike showed up one night with a cat. *"Before my husband pulled him out of his backpack, a heard a gigantic 'MEOW!' I thought to myself, 'This must be one enormous cat,' then out came this little bitty thing, and that's how he got his name, 'Thunder,'"* she chuckled.

"Sometime after that, Mike brought home a little Chi-Terrier mix named 'Kuma' that our gardener gave him. She turned out to be Thunder's best friend; they went together like peas and carrots. They got into everything together, and even shared the 'walk of shame,'" she grinned.

"*Then in the mid 1990's,*" Shell continued. "*We added a 7-month-old silver, black and tan female German Shepherd named 'Mariah.' She had no formal training for living inside, where she, unfortunately, discovered so many beautiful items to enjoy, like hats, video games, shoes, and pillows that somehow self-destructed,*" she said teasing.

"*It was trying at times, but she did get better and eventually learned how to be an 'inside dog.' You would have thought, a great watch dog too,*" she scoffed. "*Her mere size would be enough to frighten anyone off!*" she stressed. "*And maybe it would have, but I have a feeling that if anyone tried to break-in, she would just run and fetch her ball or Frisbee for them to throw for her,*" she laughed. "*As a distraction of course, while I called the police,*" Shell added facetiously.

"*When we finally got our home on the base, we were so excited, but it didn't last long,*" she said disheartened. "*We were informed that we were only allowed to have one dog,*" she said dismayed.

"*The angst I felt was sickening. I didn't know what I would do,*" she said in a worried tone. "*So, we talked to our gardener again, who had given us Kuma, and luckily their situation had changed where they were now able (and thrilled) to have her back,*" she said with relief and gratitude. "*I continued to check-in on her periodically,*" she added.

"*We were in the Philippines for three years when Mike got his orders that we were leaving. He added that we would not be able to take Thunder or Mariah,*" Shell told me, looking appalled. "*Because it would be too costly!*" she derided. "*Well, my reply came swiftly and harshly...'Hell yes!' I said. 'We are taking them!' It cost us $200 and they were worth every penny,*" she huffed with gratified.

Unfortunately, in 2001 Mike and Shell were divorced. "*It was a difficult time,*" Shell remembered. "*And I don't know what I would have done without Thunder and Mariah; they were my constant companions,*" she reminisced.

"*Mariah would lean against me (all 100 lbs) if I was crying, and Thunder would yelp loudly until I laughed through my tears. They just made my life bearable,*" she sighed.

"*Mariah was with me for only 8 short years,*" Shell lamented. "*Hardly enough time to repay her for all she had given me,*" she added, somberly. "*She became ill very quickly, and the day I drove her to the veterinarian's office, I knew she wouldn't be coming home again. I stayed with her as she slipped away,*" Shell's eyes swelled with tears.

"*The loss was tremendous; she would not be there to lean on me again. My heart was broken. My girl, my companion, was gone,*" she sighed, as she continued to fight back the tears. "*Thunder realized after a few days of yowling and searching everywhere, that her Mariah was not coming back. We were both in mourning,*" she wiped her eyes.

"*Thunder was with me for 18 wonderful years,*" Shell continued. "*And he passed while I was cradling him in my arms. I was a mess for weeks,*" she said, taking a deep breath. "*I wondered if I could ever go through this again,*" now, shaking her head. "*It would be nine years before I did.*"

Since her childhood, Shell has been deeply connected to animals in need of rescuing. After the loss of her precious pets, she was more motivated than ever to help others to find their forever home.

"*At the end of 2009, I decided I wanted to volunteer at the local shelter,*" Shell told me. "*However, before I could put my plan to work, my mom—who wrestled with many health issues at the time—was admitted to the hospital where she was put on life support.*"

When her mom's health improved enough to go home, Shell moved in to care for her, as her mom had lovingly done for her. Shell shared with me how sad and yet wonderful this time was.

They were able to share some very special memories and moments before her mom passed away at 75.

"I lost my mom, my friend, my mentor and the kindest person I ever knew," Shell shared, with tears. *"My mom's last words to me, 'Shell, go live your life, and learn to be happy again.' These are the very words that would lead me to where I am today."*

Indeed, Shell's mother's words were the catalyst for her to focus on the things that truly made her happy, such as animal rescue.

"I started to volunteer at C.A.R.L. *(Canine Adoption Rescue League) caregivers based in Ventura, CA, while continuing to work full time. I spent every moment I could there and I fell in love with rescue work...again!"* She added with emphasis.

"I was their lead dog-walker, and I attended every adoption event I could. I even inquired into full-time work there, but sadly it wasn't enough to support me. Still I decided to take two weeks off of my regular job to spend as much time as I could at the kennel, and anywhere else they needed me," she offered. *"It became a time of healing for me,"* she added with a contented smile.

"However, as fate would have it, while I was there, one of the kennel attendants told me about Best Friends Animal Society, *with lifesaving centers across the country. When I visited their website, to see what they were all about, I couldn't believe what I found. They not only rescued dogs, they had over 1,700 animals on any given day. It was like Disneyland for animals,"* she gushed. *"As I searched the job postings, I found two available positions; one for caregiver and another for volunteer lead position. I filled out the applications for both jobs and waited to hear—not telling anyone about it,"* Shell whispered.

"Well, I had two weeks off from work... so off I went," Shell said enthusiastically. *"The experience I had while there was like no other. By the end of the two-week trial visit, I had made the choice that changed my life's direction."*

"I was still healing over the loss of my mom, but I kept hearing her words in my heart," she said somberly. *"So, in 2013, I accepted the job that has changed my life. Caregiver is hard work, it's an emotional daily experience, but it's a labor of love. I'm just doing what I did for my mom, but with animals, so in some way I feel like I am honoring her,"* Shell said proudly.

"In 2014, I adopted two small dogs that came from a hoarding situation in Phoenix; forty animals all in one home," she shook her head. *"They were both part of the 14 that we rescued. Not <u>one</u> was spayed or neutered,"* Shell said in detest. *"Hence there were 40 dogs of all ages and conditions. The cutest bunch of 'littles' you have ever seen,"* her expression now turning to a smile.

"At first, I just planned to get one, 'Leilani,' a light brown chihuahua-terrier mix with the best ears and most soulful eyes I had ever seen," she gushed. *"She was known to growl if any of the other dogs annoyed her, which was quite often... still does (scary... not),"* she chuckled.

"Then there is 'Keiki,' a black and white apple head chihuahua mix with big eyes and ears like Yoda. Everyone told me, 'Oh, you have to take her, she is so sweet'—remember this for later," she winked. *"I have nicknames for them now; Leilani, I call 'LaLa' and I call Keiki, 'Manu' (and sometimes 'baby bird')."*

"I went to meet her in the clinic where she was recovering from surgery for a hernia, which had grown to the size of a baseball due to having had so many the litters. She also had an enlarged, heart and a murmur to go along with that," she added. *"She had horrible teeth when I got her as well. It was so bad, she had to have a dental visit where they had to take all but two teeth. So, poor thing, she only has the two canine teeth left. However, she has no problem gumming everything I give her,"* she snickered.

"They both love hopping and jumping up and down when food is being readied. I call it their 'dance.' They both also love sunning themselves on the window sill, watching the world roll by."

"Now, remember when I said Keiki was the sweet one? Well, 'sweet' yes, but very naughty too! She's like a goat! She will eat anything she can get to," Shell huffed.

"I came home one day to see her being very subdued, not her normal greeting. Somehow she managed to get up on the sink and had eaten three large muffins of chocolate and peach. Well, that prompted an immediate emergency visit to the veterinarians office," she said sternly. "Without going into details, Keiki was not very happy when they were done with her," she emphasized.

"Unlike LaLa, Keiki couldn't care less about loud noises, storms and thunder, but she gets very jealous whenever LaLa cozies up to me. So then, any time there is a storm or it's the 4th of July, I have two 'dog hats' on my head," she laughed. "Keiki likes to crawl on my chest, places her paws to the back of her ears, then flops them on my chest," she says gesturing with her hands to her ears. "Look-up the 'Chinese cat waving,' online and you'll see what I mean," she grinned.

"Thankfully the girls have learned to get along with other dogs," Shell nodded, confidently. "So I have been able to provide a service of doggie day care, I call it 'Chi-chi Day care.'"

"There is one dog I care for who is so adorable with a sweet personality. He loves it at my house, and I post daily stories and pictures on Facebook for his mom to see while she's gone. While the girls sun themselves at the window, he will usually sit there and stare at them as if to say, 'When is it my turn?' So, I push the ottoman over to him where he can watch out the window too."

When I asked Shell if she had any memorable stories she could share. Her eyes got big and she nodded anxiously.

"Imagine your worst nightmare and then it happens. The house I rent is quirky but with lots of charm. I was at work one day when I received a call from the owner telling me the house was on fire! Immediately I screamed, 'My dogs are in the house!' as I dropped the *phone, ran to my car, and started the 10-minute drive home that felt more like hours,"* she groaned.

"I got to the house to see firemen everywhere. The fire was out, but smoke still exuded from the roof. I yelled out to them, 'My dogs are in the house,'" she said, looking panicked.

"A fireman quickly ran into the house, located Keiki in the bedroom, and carried her out to me," Shell described with a sense of relief. But what about LaLa, I asked.

"I was told that LaLa had darted out the gate, around the corner, and down to the hotel," she said. *"So, I grabbed Keiki, jumped in the car, and started driving and yelling out the car window for LaLa."*

"While I had friends helping me in my search, someone had also called the police, who had found her and brought her to me. She was wrapped in a towel, shaking but safe," Shell shook her head in relief and with gratitude that both her puppies were safe.

"I will forever be grateful to the gentleman that saw the smoke and immediately called the fire department, as well as to the firemen who showed up and saved my girl Keiki. Thanks to them, I was able to save a lot of the house. I'm also grateful to the policeman that found LaLa and lovingly brought her to me. Thank you so much for being there!"

Curious, I asked Shell, how her house is now?

"We were able to move back into the house after all the repairs were done. Unfortunately, it took a while before the girls felt safe whenever I left them for work, but they are getting used to it and feeling safe again," she nodded. *"Keiki hated it whenever she would hear the swish noise that the gas pilot made when I turned on the stove. Then she would run out to the backyard and just stand there, violently shaking. Finally, I decided to buy a counter top convection oven to help ease her fear. It's all I use now and she is fine with that."*

What a traumatic experience! How are the dogs doing now?

"Keiki's heart problems have progressed to the next level of an enlarged heart," Shell says somberly. *"She is at the end of the level they call 'B2.' She was put on meds in November of 2018. Eventually I know this will be what takes her from me,"* she worried. *"Hopefully she won't get to 'B4' (end stage) for a few more years. I am not ready to say goodbye,"* Shell maintained. *"Until then she still dances for food, will eat anything I give her, and suns herself on the window sills with her sister by her side,"* she smiled.

"You know they cannot live forever. As a caregiver, I have been with many animals at the end of their lives due to many different illnesses; making hard decisions so they will not suffer, being there as they slowly slip away, crying, mourning them. And yet, we still would, and do, go through it again and again. I could not dream of doing anything else or being anywhere else," Shell gave a quick confident nod.

Shell told me she feels that she has honored her Mom's wishes; the fact that she took a risk to give up a life of comfortable familiarity for one full of risks of uncertainty. Yet, even though there are times when it does bring great sadness, it also comes with tremendous joy, laughter, lots of puppy licks, dog hair, and innumerable tail wags.

"Oi Kau Ka Lau E Hana Iola Honua"
("Live your life while the sun is still shining.")
~ Hawaiian Proverb

56359218R00106

Made in the USA
Middletown, DE
23 July 2019